A fairer world may only come thr

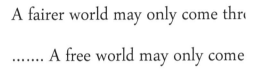....... A free world may only come

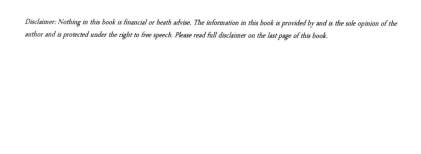
Thank you for having purchased my book, I wrote it with passion and commitment to bring you useful knowledge about bitcoin through my journey in life.

If at the end of it you will have enjoyed reading it, please leave a review on Amazon. I read every review and they help new readers discover my book.

"There is an extremely powerful force that, so far, science has not found a formal explanation to. It is a force that includes and governs all others and is even behind any phenomenon operating in the universe and has not yet been identified by us.

This universal force is LOVE.

When scientists looked for a unified theory of the universe, they forgot the most powerful unseen force.

Love is Light, that enlightens those who give and receive it.

Love is gravity, because it makes some people feel attracted to others.

Love is power, because it multiplies the best we have, and allows humanity not to be extinguished in their blind selfishness. Love unfolds and reveals.

For love we live and die.

Love is God and God is Love.

This force explains everything and gives meaning to life. This is the variable that we have ignored for too long, maybe because we are afraid of love because it is the only energy in the universe that man has not learned to drive at will.

To give visibility to love, I made a simple substitution in my most famous equation.

If instead of E = mc2, we accept that the energy to heal the world can be obtained through love multiplied by the speed of light squared, we arrive at the conclusion that **love is the most powerful force there is, because it has no limits.**

After the failure of humanity in the use and control of the other forces of the universe that have turned against us, it is urgent that we nourish ourselves with another kind of energy...

If we want our species to survive, if we are to find meaning in life, if we want to save the world and every sentient being that inhabits it, love is the one and only answer.

Perhaps we are not yet ready to make a bomb of love, a device powerful enough to entirely destroy the hate, selfishness and greed that devastate the planet.

However, each individual carries within them a small but powerful generator of love whose energy is waiting to be released.

When we learn to give and receive this universal energy, dear Lieserl, we will have affirmed that love conquers all, is able to transcend everything and anything, because love is the quintessence of life.

I deeply regret not having been able to express what is in my heart, which has quietly beaten for you all my life. Maybe it's too late to apologize, but as time is relative, I need to tell you that I love you and thanks to you I have reached the ultimate answer! ".

Your father Albert Einstein

Foreword

An idea whose time has come cannot be stopped by any army, any nation, or any pandemic!

For my profession I develop trans-catheter hearth valves, I was among the first to bring to many hospitals around the world trans-percutaneous aortic valves, a lifesaving procedure which required no open-heart surgery. Today I am lucky to develop a novel trans-cutaneous mitral valve applications which, I hope, will help many people achieve a better quality of life and a higher life expectancy.

I love science, I love learning, I love the beautiful world we live in, but mostly I love humanity and I love freedom.

As I travel the world for business, I see the same picture over and over again. People stuck in a hamster wheel which they do not know they are in and, even worse, they do not know it has been built just for them.

I meet people from all nations and walks of life, in their eyes I often see frustration and hopelessness. Zombies blind to what is really controlling and imprisoning them, walking every step of their lives trying to make ends meet, working jobs they hate and having the illusion of living in freedom, democracy and self-determination but unknowingly stuck in a purposeless, passionless, and most importantly loveless matrix.

I very often talk about bitcoin with the people I randomly meet. My audience is usually taxi drivers, waiters, physicians, nurses, cleaning people..., pretty much anyone who is friendly enough to strike a conversation with me. Occasionally, I have also talked about bitcoin to executives, investors, and bankers. However, I prefer the average every-day worker as an audience because those are the people who allow the world to function and, unfortunately, these are also the people who literally get "shafted" by the unjust and corrupt financial system we are forced to live in. More often than not, it is the working man and woman who is open to hear about how to improve their financial situation and how to acquire more freedom; and these are the people who, frankly, I care the most about.

I literally have nothing to gain from these random conversations, my only hope is that during the past years I helped someone along the way gain a better understanding of our financial world, the values of freedom, independence, and self-determination.

This is exactly the purpose of this book: help you understand what bitcoin is, at least from my own personal prospective, and how it can be used to achieve prosperity and, most importantly, true freedom. This is however not only true for people, but this book is a message to all nation-states, which may also achieve independence from the enslaving chains of international debt and prosperity for their people, by adopting bitcoin as their treasury reserve and legal tender.

In this book you will often come across the word freedom, that is because at the surface bitcoin is a money-making machine, a highly speculative risk asset... but once you really understand it..., once you really get it..., you will find out that bitcoin is there to offer a chance for freedom, peace, and equal opportunities to the world.

Understanding bitcoin is not an easy task, it took me literally years to grasp how an intangible digital asset could be of such importance. I hope that through this book you will be able to gain some understanding, at least as seen from my humble prospective.

The 2019-2023 current Covid-19 crisis has put strain not only on the world's economies, but most importantly on families, friendships, and humanity as a whole. We are divided into a terrible self-destructing tribalism, and we are so blind that most of us cannot see that we are divided by design:

"Divide et Vince" taught us the Romans.

If you analyze our recent history, we were always divided in right and left, straight or gay, republican or democrat, fascist and communist, and now vaxed and unvaxed... masked and unmasked.

The world is controlled by only a handful of people and unelected organizations of huge influence who literally see us, regular people, as nothing less than a necessary evil, cattle to be managed for their benefits. In order to control vast hordes of intelligent and potentially dangerous humans, our puppet masters make us fall in these camps which are opposites only on the surface. Our camps are meant to divide us, because divided we are weak. Division robs us of our freedom and happiness by making humans fight against each other while our masters live a lavish life made possible only by our obedient labor.

The truth is, however, that humans of any color, gender, national origin, and social status are extremely similar to each other; We all want about the same things, all have about the same desires and, for the most part, we all have good genuine intentions.

If you are a republican and genuinely try to talk to a democrat (or vice versa), try to approach the conversation in a nonjudgmental way, most likely you will see that you are very alike and only have slightly different ways to think about issues and how to go about them. I believe this to be true for the great majority of the population with only few extremists on each side which would make this statement false. The same thing will apply if you talk to a Ukrainian and a Russian, both want to live in peace and in freedom, both love their families, desire a home and an occasional vacation. Hatred is pushed on us by people and organizations which strive to divide us for their own interests and benefits.

The Covid crisis is far from over, and it is the one event that has divided us and imprisoned us as nothing else in the history of humanity. Instead of being depressed, people should understand that this is the greatest opportunity the world has ever had to awaken and to build a future of real freedom and prosperity for future generations.

Every crisis offers an opportunity, and the greatest crisis of all is also the greatest opportunity of all.

Bitcoin has been created for us in today's digital world. It offers a chance to achieve real freedom through a decentralized, incorruptible, censorship-resistance, un-confiscatable, peer-to-peer, sound monetary system. If we adopt bitcoin as individuals and nation-states, we will be able to free ourselves from the lurking dystopian technocratic totalitarianism built on FIAT paper money (soon FIAT digital money) and digital IDs which have been designed for total financial and behavioral control, for complete subservient enslavement as best described by the now infamous motto: "You will own nothing and you will be happy".

We need to Build Back Better, but not as you hear from our current politicians, who are nothing less than puppet leaders of globalist powers. Now that the elites of the world have staged their greatest attack against humanity, we have a chance to really build back better on principles of sound economic and environmental policies for the benefit of mankind and mother earth. Nothing gives us a better opportunity than bitcoin to bring peace, freedom, and prosperity to humankind.

If you want to fix the world, you have got to fix the money!

Introduction: the FIAT money system and debt money creation

Humanity has experienced many monetary resets, the last of which occurred After WW-II. With the Bretton Woods system agreement, the US dollar replaced the British Pound Sterling becoming the world's reserve currency through the international agreement of its convertibility to gold at a fix rate of $35 per ounce. This was the beginning of a short-lived monetary gold standard which was supposed to bring financial stability to the world after a devastating war which, at its root, was ignited by the German hyperinflation and the consequent rise of the Third Reich. With the gold standard, nations of the world entrusted the Federal Reserve Bank to hold their gold in exchange for market liquidity. This agreement was good until French president De Gaulle accused the United States of printing more money than they had in gold reserves to finance the Vietnam war. In early August 1971, France sent a warship to the United States with the order to repatriate French gold. A few days later the United States unilaterally abandoned the gold standard introduced at Bretton Woods, unpegging the US dollar from gold. In 1974 the United States, through its then secretary of state Henry Kissinger, agreed to militarily protect Saudi Arabia, which in return agreed to sell their oil exclusively using the US dollar, and to purchase US debt using surplus oil proceeds. This opened the era of the petrodollar, an era of US dollar world domination marked, however, by endless warfare. Today we are again at a turning point, the Federal Reserve Bank has exponentially increased the US dollar money supply, particularly since the 2008 financial crisis. In 2017 the German Bundesbank demanded the US to return their physical gold by 2020 followed by equal requests by the Bank of Austria, the Bank of Hungary, the Bank of Turkey, the Czeck National Bank and the Bank of Poland. Concomitantly, all major central banks started massive gold acquisitions. In 2019 the Bank of International Settlements, or the central bank of all central banks, changed gold's accountability to a Tier-1 asset, or equivalent to cash, in 2020 the International Monetary Fund declared a shift towards a new Bretton Woods agreement. Saudi Arabia started accepting oil payments also in Chinese Yuan and by signing a military cooperation agreement with Russia directly challenged the 1974 petrodollar agreement. The so-called BRIC nations (Brazil, Russia, India, and China) announced a new commodity-backed world reserve currency. In 2021 El Salvador announced bitcoin as legal tender with more second tier nations expected to follow. It is a time of great financial and social changes conveniently catalyzed by the Covid-19 outbreak, which maybe was not that simply coincidental but a useful catalyst.

As mentioned, until 15 August 1971, the US dollar was backed by and redeemable for gold. This guaranteed a limited inflationary monetary supply as dollar creation was restricted by the amount of gold the Federal Reserve Bank stored in its volts. This mechanism also automatically regulated the world money supply as most of all major economies were pegged to the U.S. dollar. This system guaranteed a strong market economy and balance of powers as it kept governments in check.

What is then the FIAT money system? This is actually nothing new, it is a system which allows governments to issue currencies which are not backed by gold, or are not redeemable for gold, but are only backed by the trust in the issuing government and its economic strength. It is government money by decree, a system inherently built on debt which incentivizes ever growing governments and governmental agencies, an endless state of warfare, financial neo colonialism, natural resources and human exploitation. The FIAT money system is inflationary by design and will always inevitably cause a debt bubble cycle, which will cause the end of that particular currency and will require a monetary renegotiation, a new social contract, and the birth of a new monetary system. The current Euro-dollar FIAT system is today at the end of its debt bubble. Now you see why nations are getting ready to a monetary renegotiation by amassing gold and bitcoin, and why huge societal changes are automatically leading us to a new social contract catalyzed by the Covid-19 pandemic.

As mentioned, in recent history, it was President Richard Nixon who took the United States (and the whole world) out of the gold standard and reintroduced a FIAT monetary system. The newly introduced system gave central banks the ability and flexibility to issue money without any tangible backing to more efficiently steer and control monetary policy for the "benefit" and "protection" of the people. In fact, the gold standard could not provide the necessary flexibility in monetary policy to manage recessions, expansions, inflationary and deflationary pressures, so a system was needed for modern economies to work.... or at least so the story goes. In economic academic terms, Austrian economics was replaced by the Keynesian economic theory which foresees flexible fiscal and monetary policies to achieve stable economic growth, low unemployment, and low inflation. In reality, getting rid of the gold standard allowed politicians, bankers, and strong interest groups, now in charge of the powerful printing press, to steer economic warfare, acquire enormous political and military power, and accumulate riches at the ultimate cost of the working classes. With the end of the Gold Standard, the corner stone of a truly free-market economy which could fairly and organically grow was eliminated; as a result taxation has steadily increased, interest rates have steadily decreased, debt has ballooned, governments and governmental agencies have become infinite larger.

Today's FIAT money is mostly created by governments and private banks. Private banks create money by issuing loans. In fact, any kind of loan such, as a credit card, a home mortgage, a car loan etc., is issued by a private entity after deciding that the creditor may be trusted to repay the loan back with interest. When these private banks or financial entities (who work on fractional reserves) create a new loan, the central bank electronically issues new "minted" FIAT money. Governments also indirectly create money by issuing government's debt, mostly in the form of government bonds, which are then acquired by central banks through the issuance of new liquidity.

Money so minted, is literally created as debt and out of thin air because it is not backed by gold or any other commodity with an intrinsic value; However, it must be repaid in full, with interest. Interest is the key word here, please pay attention! As money is generated by the central bank and needs to be repaid with interests to the central bank itself, how is it possible to give the central bank more money back than it initially gave if only the central bank is allowed to create it? Very simple, this is only possible if an ever-increasing quantity of loans are created in the form of both private and public debt. This is why I say that FIAT money is created as debt, and it is the biggest Ponzi scheme ever created. This system may mathematically only work for as long as the debt bubble keeps on expanding.

The FIAT money system is based on debt and is only backed by trust, or belief, in the issuing bodies and their underlying economies.

With such mechanism, central banks are able to mint money with cents on the dollar but will require repayment of the full principle plus interest with money earned (however) through real labor.

The fact that FIAT money is created as debt is the very reason that countries and private citizens are always deeper indebted, debt itself is used to buy goods and services with a currency which is designed to be continuously debased by inflation. This mechanism heavily penalizes savers and allows banks to highly leverage deposits by using a fractional reserves system; Today, for every dollar deposited, banks only have on average 3 cents in their safes making the system very fragile to insolvencies and bank runs. You often hear the term "too big to fail"; That means that if a big debtor fails to pay back its debt, it will cause a systemic domino effect which could potentially bring down the whole financial system. In fact, you have noticed that large debtors are always bailed out by governments in times of crises. You actually also hear the word "bail in", this means that financial institutions' depositors are now required to help banks cover their unpaid debt in case of critical insolvencies through their own deposits.

You see now why financial scandals like the Lehman Brothers' collapse in 2008 can cause debt defaults and chain reactions with the potential of bringing down the whole financial system and why bank runs would cause the same problem.

To avoid the collapse of such a fragile system, it is absolutely necessary that the public narrative is strictly controlled, and that people are reassured by things such as FDIC deposit insurance, which would in reality only protect savers if a small bank were to go out of business, but it would never withstand the magnitude of a structural banking collapse.

This is the reason why countries need an ever-increasing level of societal control, and why strict capital controls and restrictions on cash are so starkly enforced. This is also the very reason why the world is moving as fast as possible towards centralized digital currencies, which will warrant control by default.

This kind of system guarantees that it is just a matter of time until, yet another FIAT debt cycle will come to an end, as history has shown time and time again.

Maybe it will be another financial scandal, a war, or a pandemic which will act as a catalyst to bring the system down and lead to a new financial reset, but the truth is that the system has been built to be needing a periodic reset. The elites will always come on top because they know how to play the game while regular people will always pay the consequences. Today's great reset is a financial necessity whose roots go back to 15 August 1971 and the end of the Bretton Woods agreement system.

The reality is that you are given monopoly paper money, while central banks keep on hoarding gold and some, have started hoarding bitcoin.

As you noticed, I started the book talking about the FIAT money system. This is necessary as we first need to have at least a basic knowledge of how the money we use today is created before we can even venture in understanding bitcoin.

With the FIAT money system and the fractional reserve banking, the greatest Ponzi scheme in history has been created and we are all sitting on an ever-increasing debt bubble which will eventually need deleveraging.

Historically, deleveraging has always been accomplished through wars, coups, and violent revolutions. Today is no different, but warfare has deeply evolved and has become asymmetric; it includes not only armed conflicts, but also biological, psychological, information, financial and cyber-warfare.

You are in the midst of a war, but many of us do not know that it is happening and that its root cause is mostly financial.

Chapter one: What is bitcoin?

When I first encountered bitcoin, I asked myself exactly this very question: What is it?

I am sure that you have asked yourself this question as well many times and maybe you think you know the answer, but when your friends ask you about it, you find it difficult to give a satisfactory explanation. If that is the case, this is exactly how I felt when I first bought bitcoin. I had some basic concepts such as the 21 million maximum number of bitcoin which may ever be minted, or that it is a block chain but having a solid understanding of what bitcoin really is, is not that easy. In fact, it took me a very long time to have a good grasp on it.

I remember that during my early bitcoin days I used to answer this question just by repeating: "Bitcoin is a digital currency based on a decentralized blockchain with a limited supply". Then, hoping for no further questions, I would always add, trying to impress my audience: " ...I made $20,000 just during the past 6 months!!".

The truth was that at the beginning I really did not know what I bought into, I only cared that it was making me more FIAT money. People who remain at this very basic level of knowledge, usually bail out with the first 50% bitcoin crash they experience and miss out on the best asset ever existed, an asset that is not only a way to escape financial slavery but is also a true beacon of freedom and hope.

I firmly believe that most people who own bitcoin do not understand in depth what bitcoin really is as it often used as a high-risk, high-return speculative asset.

So, let's go back to the question, what is bitcoin? The answer is not that trivial, so let's go step by step.

As a starter, I strongly recommend you read the bitcoin peer-to-peer e-cash white paper, which was released to the cypher-punks community on October 31st, 2008 and can still be found here:

https://bitcoin.org/bitcoin.pdf

An interesting day to release the paper! Surely, not that casually chosen.

Going back to the question, let me try to give you my best answer to this non-trivial question before diving into the rabbit hole:

Bitcoin is first and foremost a monetary ledger, hence information of how work (energy) is transferred to generate economic activity. This information is accurate, cash-final and has extremely low latency as it is transmitted at the speed of light.

Bitcoin, the asset, is digital electronic cash, created and protected by CPU power and energy. It constitutes the hardest digital asset which can ever be created on earth.

Bitcoin, the asset, is money (think of money as energy which may be spent to create economic activity) which may be owned, saved, and spent in a permissionless, incorruptible, and censorship-resistant way.

Bitcoin is a decentralized network safeguarded by miners and nodes allowing for peer-to-peer, cash-final, free, and instant payments across borders at the speed of light.

Bitcoin is humanity's true hope for freedom and peace.

Before I explain what I just wrote, let me first give you some facts:

- Satoshi Nakamoto, who released bitcoin to the world in early 2009, is an unknown figure who wrote on the forum bitcointalk.org until he disappeared. Satoshi's coins, remain as of today, still unmoved (about 1.1 million bitcoin).

- The creator of bitcoin cannot be politically and legally attacked as does not exist.

- There is a distinction between bitcoin the asset and the bitcoin the network:
  - The asset is the minted digital coin itself.
  - The network is the rails upon which bitcoin travels peer-to-peer and is made of thousands of independent miners and nodes.

- Bitcoin has a limited supply of 21 million coins which are minted at a pre-programmed inflation rate. Every four years the amount of bitcoin granted per block-reward is cut in half. Many think that this is just a way to make the coins more valuable by shrinking the supply, however it goes much deeper than that. A controlled money supply is the basis of the so called Austrian economic theory, which foresees little government intervention and a truly free and organically strong market economy as taught by Adam Smith. This is in stark contrast to the Keynesian economic theory, thought in all major universities and widely practiced today throughout the world, which foresees strong government intervention in both monetary and fiscal policies to drive economic growth and stability.

- Every bitcoin is made of 100 million Satoshis (or Sats), the last Satoshi will probably be minted in year 2140 and will cost billions of today's FIAT US dollars in energy and CPU power to mine.

- A bitcoin miner uses CPU power and energy to solve complex mathematical problems for which it is rewarded freshly minted bitcoin and fees. The more CPU power joins the network, the harder the mathematical problems become, and the more energy is required.

- The mining difficulty (hash rate) is adjusted so that one block is released about every 10 minutes. The more miners are at work at any given time, the higher the hash rate and the higher the network's security.

- Transactions are registered in blocks, which are nothing other than a public ledger. Blocks are chained to each other (from here the word blockchain) so that all transactions ever occurred are registered and viewable by anyone through a node.

- Every block has the size of 1-MB, this makes it possible for almost anyone with a normal computer to run a node.

- The bitcoin network is extremely secure in its simplicity and has never been successfully hacked.

Now that you have some basics, let's get into the rabbit hole!

As Satoshi talked about creating an e-cash system, let's start with the concept of cash!

Cash guarantees ownership, trust, independence, and a certain degree of privacy because cash allows for peer-to-peer transactions. If you would like to buy a sweater from John down the street, and John is willing to part from it for $5, you meet John and you give him the $5 bill. John would check that the bill is real, would put the bill in his pocket, and hand you his sweater. As you handed the bill to John the monetary property automatically changed from you to John and you both completed a financial transaction without any intermediary, yet with trust that the buyer was receiving the property of the $5 bill.

What happens now if you want to buy a similar sweater online from someone who goes by the name of "Pete76" and lives 1,000 miles away from you? Or what happens if you simply go to a store and buy an item for which you would like to pay electronically in a peer-to-peer cash-final transaction? As you both do not know and trust each other, how can you complete a financial transaction where no trust is guaranteed between the parties and without any intermediary? Sure, you can use a credit card, bank wire or services such as PayPal, but all these modalities involve a third party necessary to overcome trust. Using a third party, however, comes at the cost of ownership, privacy, independence, censorship resistance and confiscability, which are all fundamental properties of cash. To solve the problem Satoshi created bitcoin, a peer-to-peer digital cash system. But how would you create such a system in a way that ownership, trust, peer-to-peer independence, and privacy would be granted? Satoshi created bitcoin the asset and bitcoin the network. The asset is the coin (the asset or stored economic energy), and the network is the payment system which guarantees ownership, decentralization, security, peer-to-peer transactions, censorship resistance and inconfiscability at a pre-programmed inflation rate.

Ownership is simply granted by the fact that the owner of the coin possesses private digital keys. These keys, like the keys of a car, allow only the rightful owner of coins to dispose of them and are so secure that, so far, the network was never successfully hacked or, in bitcoin gibberish, it never generated a double spend event. Using more bitcoin gibberish, private keys are cryptographically generated by a list of 12 or 24 random words through an elliptic curve digital signature algorithm. Through this cryptographic mechanism Satoshi created a system that would prevent double spending, or using the same coin to make two distinct payments. Proof of the bitcoin's system security are Satoshi's coins themselves; they remain unmoved although worth a fortune as only Satoshi, or someone with his private keys, is allowed to use those funds.

Decentralization: The network is composed of independent miners and nodes. Miners use their CPU power and electricity to solve mathematical problems under a decentralized consensus mechanism called proof-of-work; As miners compete against each other to solve these problems, they get rewarded with freshly minted bitcoin which are allowed to come into circulation on a pre-programmed inflation schedule. As the value of the coins increases, more miners are encouraged by pure economics to join the network by providing additional CPU power, or hash rate. As the available hash rate increases so does the difficulty of the mathematical problems and the amount of CPU power and electricity required. In other words, as more computers compete for a fixed amount of available coins, more work is required in a process which is similar to mining physical gold, from here the word "bitcoin mining".

This system gives bitcoin both security and intrinsic value!

The fact that miners may join the network from anywhere in the world, and that proof-of-work is required to mint new coins, allows for mining decentralization and for an automatic coins' distribution because miners are forced to sell at least some of their freshly minted coins to cover their high operating costs.

Miners not only mint new bitcoin, but also compete to confirm financial transactions in order to guarantee that when a person sends funds to another person, those funds are legitimate, and that ownership is transferred. In fact, every transaction needs to be confirmed by 6 independent miners and is documented on a so-called block, which is a simple public ledger. Miners are rewarded with a fee for confirming each transaction. A new block is released about every 10 minutes, all blocks are chained to each other, hence the word block-chain. Nodes keep a copy of all transactions ever executed on the block-chain network. As each block is only 1-MB in size, almost anyone can run a node, this guarantees that thousands of computers all over the world keep a copy of all transactions ever transmitted over the network for the sake of transparency.

Miners and nodes provide security and decentralization for the network. Decentralization is a key point as it guarantees that no single entity has control over the network and its monetary policy, it keeps the system honest and does not allow for private interests to act at the cost of the community.

Now that we have explained what bitcoin is and how the decentralized network has been set up, let's go back to our transaction between you and "Pete76". Through the bitcoin network you may now send "Pete76" $5 worth of bitcoin by using a so-called public address, which is just a sequence of letters and numbers generated by your private keys, this is a little bit like using an email address but just longer. Once "Pete76" receives your bitcoin, he becomes owner of the coin as the transfer of ownership has been verified by 6 independent miners. The change in ownership is registered on the public ledger, or block, and may be audited by anyone running a node.

This transaction has been performed through a peer-to-peer exchange of monetary electronic property which is cash final without the use of an intermediary.

The last box that needs to be checked is trust. How can Peter trust that the bitcoin he received had not been spent already for something else before it got to him? In other words, how can the system prevent double spending? Trust is achieved by the fact that tricking the system is more expensive than being honest, let me explain how this is done and please pay close attention because this explains bitcoin's need of ever-increasing amounts of energy and CPU power.

If a miner wants to trick the system, it will have to re-write history, in other words it will have to write on the block that the funds you sent to "Pete76" were in actuality sent to "Mia92". To do so, the dishonest miner needs to divert the funds to a different public address which is connected to "Mia92's" private key. However, other miners would see the dishonesty and override it. In other words, the dishonest miner has done the work to confirm the transaction, but because the confirmation was wrong it spent CPU power and energy without getting any reward.

However, there is a way for re-writing history forcefully on the bitcoin blockchain, and this is called a 51% attack. What this means is that the majority of the available CPU power would have to coalize to dishonestly rewrite a block. This would mean that any new block who came after the one you would want to cheat would have to be re-written at the expense of the majority of CPU power in the network and at the cost of all electricity needed to do the work. This attack, if at all possible, would today cost tens of billion dollars in equipment and energy, and would require the extremely unlikely agreement of the majority of the miners. Furthermore, such an attack would render the bitcoin network useless and therefore worthless. Who would run such an expensive attack knowing that the stolen coins would be rendered worthless? The answer is that only nation states would have the motive and the capability of running an operation of this scale and magnitude, however, such an attack is not only extremely unlikely and expensive, but it could be neutralized and backfire on the perpetrators. In fact, if such an attack were to be tried and failed, bitcoin would cement its invulnerability and become even stronger in the public eye.

What I just explained to you is the reason why bitcoin needs CPU power and energy to mint coins and keep the network running. There is no other way to keep a monetary network completely decentralized, guarantee ownership, peer-to-peer transactions, and intrinsic value in a way that it cannot be successfully attacked. Yes, systems can be designed to allow for the use of less energy and faster/cheaper transactions, thousands of networks have already done it, but this will always come at the cost of complete and full decentralization; In fact, these other networks, commonly called Alt-Coins, will in a way or another, never meet all requirements needed for a digital-gold decentralized monetary system which bitcoin pretends to be. This is not to say that all other crypto is junk and only bitcoin may be trusted, there are legitimate projects (although extremely few) who serve various purposes successfully and may have a bright future, but none of them represent digital gold like bitcoin does, none of them represent hard, sound money in a digital form.

Just like physical gold requires machinery, labor, and energy to be mined and represents hard, sound analog-physical money, bitcoin requires CPU power and energy to give security and intrinsic value to hard, sound digital money.

Bitcoin is quite literally energy transformed into digital monetary power through CPU computational work, bitcoin is private digital property which will not be diluted, and which may be transferred in time and space.

Let me try to explain this concept differently by using an analogy. The work you perform, for example in building a house or giving a haircut, is the result of transformed energy. Think about it, your labor comes from the energy given to your body by the food you ate, which in turn comes from the energy used to raise an animal, grow vegetables, and process it. Which always comes from the energy of the sun! Everything you do ultimately comes from the energy of the sun transformed into a different state. In these terms, the money you receive in exchange for your labor is stored energy under the form of a banknote. This banknote may be redeemed for goods and services which, as we just saw, are nothing else than transformed energy through work. Unfortunately, you are no longer given money backed by gold, but you are given fake paper FIAT money printed out of thin air which is intrinsically inflationary in nature; using different words, the value of the banknote is always quickly and strongly diluted by inflation. This is true in every country which uses FIAT money; Inflation may be lower or higher depending on where you live, but your FIAT money is unavoidably worth less and less with every passing day.

As the money you worked for is diluted in time by inflation, some of that stored energy is not lost (as energy is never created or destroyed by always just transformed) but is literally (and silently) transferred to the government and other private interests. With bitcoin, you have the option to transform your energy into digital hard money created and protected by CPU power, energy and a decentralized monetary system with a limited supply. In fact, the proof-of-work protocol which bitcoin uses, requires huge amount of computational power and energy to preserve the stability, honesty and security of the system. When you exchange your FIAT money into bitcoin, or better said, when you exchange your work for bitcoin, you are now conserving your work into energy which can be moved at the speed of light in time and space. Nobody can dilute your work, nobody can prevent you from using your bitcoin to buy goods and services, nobody can prevent you from saving your work through time without losing your work to inflation (the silent thief), nobody will ever be allowed to change the rules which you originally accepted when you bought into the bitcoin system. Besides inflation, money moving through third parties, such as a bank or a credit card financial institution, may be easily restricted. The fact that you need to ask permission, or show proof of innocence, to use your money is a de facto weaponization of the financial system which has been introduced slowly and silently over the past decades and has reached restriction levels which should now worry even the average citizen, who unfortunately has become completely anesthetized to basic concepts of freedom, independence, and self-reliance.

When I say to people that bitcoin is stored digital energy, I get really baffled reactions, but if you understand this principle, you understand bitcoin.

Let me spend a few words on privacy. Bitcoin, contrary to the belief of many is not a secret transaction but only a private transaction. Every single bitcoin transaction is recorded on-chain and can be tracked. To associate the transaction to a physical person all it is needed is to associate the public keys used for the transaction to a physical person. This is a little hard to do but not that impossible. Bitcoin is not secretive by design; it was never meant to be money to conduct secret business, although it has been used for this purpose in the past and it will be used so in the future by people who ignore this fact.

Bitcoin was designed for peer-to-peer private transactions of digital sound money the same way as cash is designed for peer-to-peer private transactions of analog money.

In conclusion, bitcoin is energy stored in digital monetary form! The bitcoin monetary system cannot be changed for political advantage or economic theft and is built upon an unchangeable software code in cyber space, protected by CPU power (miners and nodes) and energy (electricity).

The fact that the bitcoin's dollar price strongly fluctuates, and we will analyze the historical price charts later, is only a short-term speculative effect dictated by the young and disruptive nature of this technology, speculation, and the fact that in most countries bitcoin is not yet legal tender. Therefore, the USD valuation fluctuations have only a short-term relative meaning and have nothing to do with bitcoin's intrinsic value which derives from the fact that it is energy and CPU power digitally stored as hard, sound digital money.

In physics terms I like to define bitcoin as conservation of work or economic energy.

One other aspect of money in general, hence of bitcoin, is that money is pure economic information. The smallest the latency (or the time it takes for information to travel) and the smallest the error the higher is its monetary value. As money is a tool to exchange work, or economic energy, it is precious data of supply and demand; it represents what people need, want, and do in contrast to by what is economically offered.

Bitcoin's blockchain contains all this data, it stores it in eternity and accurately, and through the Lightning Network it is information transferred at the speed of light.

For more information about bitcoin, visit https://bitcoin.org (I have no affiliation with bitcoin.org)

Chapter two: What is money, what should it be, and what makes of bitcoin the best form of money

Now that we have a better understanding of the FIAT money system and of bitcoin, let's ask ourselves some fundamental questions:

What is money? What should money be? How would bitcoin provide the solution?

Question no.1, What is money?

In traditional terms money is a medium of exchange, a unit of account and a store of value; however, it is a tool to exchange value, promote economic activity and shape social behavior. Through its weaponization, it is also used for economic warfare and for the exploitation of people and resources.

When economies were still rudimentary, people used to barter. If I had a cow and I needed a jacket, I would go down to the market and tried to exchange my milk for clothing. This of course worked as far as the person making the jacket needed milk and was willing to trade his jacket for my milk. Of course, if I wanted to trade my milk for a knife, but the person who sold knives needed a horse, then the trade was de-facto impossible. In order to facilitate trade, people started adopting money as a medium of exchange. Initially money was made of special objects which had a limited supply, then as humanity advanced, people went from objects to gold and silver coins, to banknotes, checks, credit cards, digital wiring and now you can exchange resources using a digital device such as a phone. Soon we will also have central bank digital currencies (CBDCs), which represent the ultimate evolution of money, although about this last point I would like to reserve a special chapter.

Money then, throughout its historic evolution, is a medium which facilitates exchange in economies which are always more fluid, interconnected and complex. As such it can be considered as a tool for economic energy to move goods between buyers and sellers.

Money is also a unit of account as things are priced as a currency value within the same jurisdiction.

The third definition of *money is store of value*. In strong economies with stable currencies, this is somewhat true for the short and medium term. A pair of shoes would cost me $100 today and if I save the $100 bill, maybe (and with a little luck), I could buy the same pair of shoes a year later for the same amount, in this case I can save money as a mean of storing value. Of course, in more unstable economies such as Argentina (Argentina is just an example, the list is extremely long!), with much weaker currencies affected by strong inflation, money is not a store of value even in the short term.

Bitcoin meets all the traditional definitions of money as it is the perfect medium of exchange: It is divisible down to 100.000.000 Satoshi (100M Satoshi = 1 BTC) and may be transferred peer-to-peer at the speed of light, bitcoin is a unit of account as long as things may be priced in bitcoin (or satoshis), and bitcoin is also the perfect store of value because of its limited supply and pre-designed minting schedule.

There are two common objections which people make about bitcoin as a medium of exchange and a unit of account, both are valid and are worth a discussion:

The first objection is that bitcoin's price is too volatile to make it a medium of exchange. I agree that bitcoin is too volatile in its USD valuation, but this is due to the fact that bitcoin is not legal tender in most countries and to the fact that it is a young, disruptive asset and technology still in a price discovery phase. Its USD valuation is also heavily affected by short term speculation. It is worth to note, however, that if bitcoin is priced in other currencies such as the Argentinian Peso or the Turkish lira, then its volatility on the downside almost disappears.

The second objection is that for every-day purchases, particularly for small-ticket items such as a cup of coffee, transferring bitcoin is too slow and expensive. This is true for as long as all transactions are on-chain, but today this is no longer a valid argument because of the adoption of layer two solutions such as the Lightning Network®, which allows for instant, frictionless, and almost free transactions across the globe.

There are however other properties of money which transcend traditional definitions. Money is information, it contains data on how and for what value is transferred and how energy is allocated to produce work. The accuracy and speed in collecting and transferring data and energy is key to improve economic activity. Here bitcoin excels as it's blockchain offers instant and transparent data and layer two solutions such as the Lightning Network offer instant, frictionless and almost free exchanges. To understand bitcoin, although it is useful to understand the traditional definition of money, we have to shift our understanding's paradigm. Money is a tool to collect information, store and trade economic value, and transfer economic energy through time and space. No form of money is perfect, even gold which has been money for thousands of years has its downfalls; bitcoin has shortcomings deriving from the fact that it is not (mostly) legal tender and it's therefore volatile for everyday purchases, it cannot be easily comprehended as is in an invisible digital form, however adoption and education will sort its shortcomings out.

If we look at bitcoin in all its features, it is the best form of money ever created not only because it fits its traditional definition, but because it offers the solution to many problems and creates new ways to make this tool, money, more effective and valuable.

Question no. 2, What is the problem with the current monetary system?

The main problem of the current monetary system is the excessive money supply and the resulting inflation, but also the rampant quest for complete governments' control which are slowly but surely weaponizing our financial systems, outlawing cash and introducing ever more effective and stringent financial controls, not only to curb illegal activities but also to shape human behavior and to foster international warfare and human exploitation.

Money supply determines the intrinsic value of money itself. Inflation is by definition an increase in money supply greater than the increase in economic value output.

I heard an interesting story one day; European traders traveled to a far pacific island and observed that the local indigenous people were trading using stone coins, which were rare on that island. They then traveled to a different island and noticed that there were plenty of those same stone coins there, so they picked up the stones from that island and spent them on the first island. By doing so they inflated the local currency, which caused a collapse of the local economy, and enslaved the local population. In this example it is not only clear how inflation robs people of economic energy, but how money as a financial instrument may be weaponized and used to exploit entire nations.

The problem of every monetary system humanity has ever created is that the temptation to deflate it by debasement is just too big to resist. Every single monetary system ever created collapsed, and its collapse was followed by the end of that civilization.

The principle is very simple, If I have $100.000 dollars' worth of assets in country X, I need $100.000 worth of money to represent this economy. If I am the imaginary king of this economy and I print an extra $10.000 of money but I did not produce 10% real extra value in the economy, I have diluted the value of the current money supply and created inflation without real economic growth. In fact, the price of all assets and goods would naturally increase by 10% to represent the actual existing money supply. In such a system, imbalances are created, and wealth is transferred unjustly and uneconomically through political power. The working savers are the ones paying the most and this can be seen by the impossibility of always more people all over the world to make ends meet, growing income inequalities, neo financial colonialism, the depletion of natural and human resources through monetary manipulation, and financial warfare.

Unfair, unjustified, and uncontrolled money supply creates inflation which has always destroyed every single currency ever created. Even the currencies which are today still standing, such as the U.S. dollar and the British Pound, have lost over 99% of their purchasing power since their inception. The fall of the current FIAT monetary system is only a question of when and how, not of if.... It is just history riming with itself, today a reset is badly needed. The fall of the current debt-based system is already occurring through inflation and deleveraging, this reset may look different than previous ones thanks to complex financial-technological tools such as the introduction of the CBDCs, but the end result will be the same.

Inflation, wars, and enslavement are very often, if not always, the results of monetary debasement and the need to reset the financial system to start a new debt cycle.

Historically, as already mentioned, no currency issuer has ever survived the temptation to supply more money than justly necessary, because the temptation to gain power through financial manipulation has always been just too strong to resist.

Slowly but surely, money printing brings to currency devaluation, inequality, and the end of a country, an empire or even an entire civilization.

The United States of America, built by a revolution in 1776 upon principles of freedom and liberty, albeit at the cost of the genocide of a great portion of its indigenous population, became the greatest empire the world has ever seen upon principles of freedom, liberty, and property rights. At the end of WW-II the US dollar became the global reserve currency and was backed by gold; Many elderly people still remember that gold was redeemable for dollars at the time. At one point the US first stopped allowing the redemption of dollars for gold (even countries could no longer redeem their own gold), then even confiscated all gold from its own citizens and started debasing the world currency.

As we have already seen, under Richard Nixon, the US detached its economy all together from the gold standard allowing the Federal Reserve to print money unhinged from its gold reserves. To truly understand the magnitude of what happened, you have to know that the Federal Reserve, officially born in 1913, is a cartel of private banks which secretly organized at Jekyll Island in 1910 to protect private banking interests. With the end of the gold standard in 1971, the US allowed a private bank cartel to legally print money out of thin air and to lend it out with interest.

Slowly, year after year, the US debased the dollar until today, when even under strong price gauging and manipulation, it takes about $1,800 to buy an ounce of gold when it used to only take $35 in 1971.

As the U.S. was able to freely print dollars, the price of gold in USD strongly increased as a direct result of the increase in money supply as shown in the USD-Gold evaluation chart below.

(Source: https://www.gold.org/goldhub/data/gold-prices)

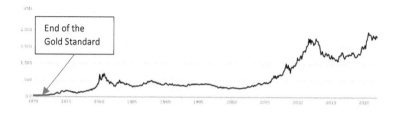

In the graph below, you can see growth in the M3-money supply since 1960 courtesy of Mr. John Williams. (Source: *www.shadowstats.com*, *Issue 1459*).

Please keep in mind that money supply accounting has changed many times over time and is quite a complex subject. If you need more information visit www.shadowstats.com (no association)

Graph 25: ShadowStats Ongoing Money Supply M3 Estimate (1960 to February 2021)

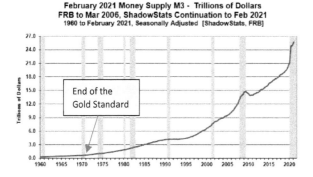

Graph 26: ShadowStats Ongoing M3 Estimate, Year-to-Year Change (1960 to February 2021)

In this contest, it is also interesting to see the median home price index in the United States since 1970.

(Source: https://dqydj.com/historical-home-prices/)

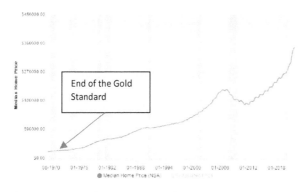

It is evident to me that with the decoupling of the US dollar from Gold, the price of gold (think of gold as real money) and the price of homes (a tangible asset everyone needs) all tremendously increased, but did they? Or is it just that the US dollar is able to buy always less goods?

If in 1971 $38 dollars bought you 1 Oz. of Gold and today you need $1,860 for the same gold coin, since 1971 in "gold" terms the US dollar has lost 98% of its value.

If in 1971 the average home cost $26,000 and today the same home costs on average $345,000, since 1971 in "home" terms the US dollar has lost 93% of its value.

Many people I know cheer to the fact that their home has lately increased so much in value but there is really nothing to cheer about. The true value of homes has probably only modestly increased depending on the kind of home and location, the truth is that average home prices have mostly been ballooned by inflation making owning a home for future generations close to impossible as average wages for the middle class have not at all matched the pace of real assets' price appreciation.

The main problem of the FIAT money system is then inflation, which is caused (as we have seen) by an excessive growth in money supply fueled by greed, corruption, political power, and war at the cost of the working classes.

How much inflation do we have? The most common measure of inflation is the CPI (consumer price index), calculated by the government and sold by the state/corporate media propaganda as holy scripture. That number is, however, only correct if you consume exactly the products in the CPI's calculated basket. For my son, who lives on Domino's Pizzas and Netflix streaming, prices never go up, his CPI is then about 0%; however, my personal yearly CPI is today anywhere between 15% and 30%. That is because my CPI basket is made of his college tuition, healthcare products, good quality clothes, real estate, a good safe new car, jewelry, healthy foods, S&P 500 stocks and of course bitcoin.

Inflation is a vector as it is dependent on what you buy. The CPI index, in its simple arithmetic one-fits-all formula, is not representative of a diverse, interconnected and extremely complex economy. Furthermore, the CPI basket is constantly updated to better reflect people's habits, or...... to best fit the government's narrative if allow me to be non-politically correct and straight out honest with you.

Let me share you yet another chart which I also picked from www.shadowstats.com showing both the official and the Shadowstats' CPI index.

(source: www.shadowstats.com, Issue 1459).

The above chart clearly shows that since the dollar was decoupled from gold, the average real inflation rate in the US has been much higher than officially reported, although this chart shows just an average and, again, is not representative of our individual needs. However, it is interesting to see that in the decade between 2010 and 2020, while the official has trended at about the 2% rate which is the FED's mission, a different accounting shows that inflation has been on average 10%. If you did not make on average 10% more money per year during this past decade, you should have observed your standards of living to have fallen, your personal debt to have increased or both.

In understanding how the CPI index is calculated there is a caveat that is worth talking about. The CPI index follows the average baskets of goods people buy, so if ribeye steaks become very expensive and people buy less stakes and more ground beef, then the CPI basket is adapted to what people actually buy, but there is no mention of the fact that people no longer buy steaks because they just can no longer afford them. Another caveat is that in the past 30 years production has been moved from the western world to mainly Asia. As people buy more and more of these goods produced in low-income countries, inflation is masked by exporting manufacturing abroad without considering that well paid manufacturing jobs are lost and without considering the heavy environmental costs that this has caused. From this you can see how decoupling from the gold standard has directly and indirectly allowed an impoverishment of the middle class, the enrichment only of the very few and the deterioration of the environment.

Another creative way to measure inflation is the yearly growth of the S&P 500 index. The index represents to me the true cost of capital. How much more does it cost me to buy a piece of our economy?

Here is another chart I would like to show you: S&P 500 index since the early 1970's

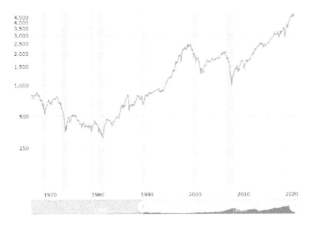

If the S&P 500 index cost me $600 in 1971 and $4,600 today, in S&P500 terms I need about 7.6 times as many dollars to buy the same piece of the U.S. economy, or in S&P 500 therms the USD has lost 87% of its value.

Let me be honest and clear to you as the reader, the data I just showed you is not meant to be a PhD work and precise to the 1%..., so if you want to argue about the method of calculation and the exact values, please be my guest; It is however irrefutable, and this the point I want to make, that there is a correlation between the end of the gold standard, the parabolic increase in money supply and the parabolic increase in the cost of tangible assets.

The picture would not be complete if we did not look at the other side of the equation: wages.

As we analyze the data, we notice that while the cost of hard assets has increased parabolically since the end of the Gold Standard, wages have only grown in a similar fashion for the top 5% of the workforce while the median wages' growth has been relentlessly slow. The bottom incomes have even been completely stagnant.

With the end of the Gold Standard and the end of real money, a huge wealth transfer has happened from the working class to the top 20% and in particular to the top 5% of the population and the government. The main reason for the wealth transfer is that the top income brackets have used cheap capital to buy and generate real assets, while the middle and lower class have just worked for money to survive, have saved cash instead of buying assets or, worse, have used high-interest lines of credit to buy consumer goods. Governments, on the other hand, were able to print money through debt creation, relentlessly increased taxes, and used inflation to increase even further their income. If you notice, every single government apparatus has become much larger since the end of the gold standard.

This chart (source: www.advisorperspectives.com), shows clearly that wages for the bottom 80% of the population has not kept up with the price of assets. There is a clear increasing divide in standards of living and de facto, the working class has transferred wealth to the top minority. This is mostly due to the FIAT money debt system, which gives asymmetric advantage to the people "closer to the printing press" and to the higher classes who are able to use money to buy real tangible assets and leaves the rest of the population behind living pay-check to pay-check.

Why do governments always end up printing too much money? This is very simple, if governments need money they have only two options, they can tax citizens or they can print it. Governments do tax citizens at an ever-increasing scale, however it comes a point where it is much easier, and politically convenient, to raise money by debasing the currency instead of taxing citizens and cause a political backlash. Inflation is hidden taxation; Inflation is the silent thief who comes at night and robs you blind. Inflation is a wealth transfer from the working class to the government and the very rich as only the few can profit from it by using political favor and resources. The working class, the average Joe, inevitably ends up on the losing end of the table because of lack of understanding and lack of access to cheap capital.

In conclusion, the main problem of the FIAT money system is excess inflation as governments' temptation to use the printing press is just too great to resist.

There are of course other problems with the current FIAT monetary system, such as inclusion, speed and cost of payment, counterfeited money, excessive government control and oversight, censorship, confiscatability etc..., but the main problems, the elephants in the room, are inflation caused by excessive money printing, government overreach to control and shape social behaviors, and international financial weaponizations for political, warfare and exploitation purposes.

While inflation keeps the current money from acting as a store of value, the slow disappearance of cash will de-facto deprive us of the possibility to make peer-to-peer transactions and will severely hinder our privacy and freedom.

While inflation dilutes our work, because of the always tighter governmental control, freedom is becoming increasingly problematic as with the FIAT money system, we must rely on third parties for any financial transaction and cash, the only way we could make p2p transactions, is already strongly restricted and is becoming increasingly inconvenient to use.

Question no. 3, How does bitcoin fix the problem of inflation, control, P-2-P payments, financial weaponization and exploitation?

We have discussed what money is and what the problems with the current monetary system are: Inflation, unequal rules for different classes of citizens, centralization of powers, privacy, limited P-2-P payments options, non-financial inclusion, censorship, confiscation, counterfeit, difficult and long cross border payments, growing economic inequalities, lack of privacy, politically motivated financial sanctions, assets freeze, human and environmental exploitation.. etc.

How does bitcoin propose to fix all this? ....and can it fix it?

The answers are within Bitcoin's core values. Each core value alone does not make of bitcoin the "better" money, but all together they do. Actually, once you get into the rabbit hole, you will realize that Bitcoin is THE only money in a digital world, the same way as gold is the only money in an analog world. Bitcoin, however, is NOT just a digital form of analog money, it redefines what money is and what money can do, it constitutes a true paradigm shift. The paradigm shift we just mentioned is the reason why bitcoin is so difficult for many people to understand.

Inflation: The bitcoin mining schedule has been written in cyberspace and cannot be modified, it allows for 21M coins to be minted through energy and computer power till the year 2140. No one, no matter how powerful, can debase bitcoin by inflation and rob the world of its economic energy. With bitcoin you may save the sweat of your brows as digital monetary energy.

Network's decentralization: the decentralization of the network constituted by miners and nodes ensures that the system will run no matter what happens in a particular nation or part of the world. We have seen this in practicality in 2021 when China shut down mining, the bitcoin network continued to work just fine, and more mining power quickly appeared in other parts of the planet. Actually, I have been getting "wind" that even with the complete ban, some Chinese miners are still operating in secret. Decentralization of CPU power guarantees resilience and fairness. Paraphrasing the great teacher Andreas Antonopoulos (no association): it is Rules without rulers!

Intrinsic Value: The fact that bitcoin requires CPU power and energy gives it intrinsic value in stark contrast to FIAT money, which is based on debt and trust.

Transferability: Value may be transferred instantaneously at the speed of light anywhere in the world as a P-2-P cash-final transactions using the bitcoin (lightning) network. The bitcoin network can take care of both remittances and payments in a way no bank and no company can because it is literally instantaneous, it is almost free, does not care about borders and jurisdictions, is P-2-P and cash final, it is censorship resistance, and it cannot be confiscated.

Transparency: All final transactions are recorded on the blockchain, these records may be read, queried, and audited by anyone running a node, yet a certain degree of privacy is guaranteed as the personal identities of the participants in the exchange are expressed as a bitcoin public address. Bitcoin blockchain records guarantee that information about economic activity is stored and available for the benefit of all participants, but it is not built with the purpose of conditioning and controlling people's economic activity, a stark difference when compared to the latest governmental digital efforts.

Censorship resistance: With the 2022 peaceful Truckers' protest in Canada, we have seen how easy it is for tyrannical governments to fight its opposition by freezing their financial resources. Taking this particular instance (although banking freezes for political reasons are nothing new), the Canadian government froze over 10M CAD raised through multiple online platforms in what clearly seemed an attempt to curb and punish political opposition, money which was lawfully and generously donated to peaceful protesters. To add insult to injury a politically-motivated hacker conveniently exposed all donors of the GoFundMe campaign and allowed the "democratic" government of Canada to also freeze private citizens' bank accounts guilty of having made a donation to support the freedom's convoy movement. This was clearly weaponizing of money for opposing political opposition!

Using the bitcoin network, funds may be transferred P-2-P in a censorship-resistant way. If I wanted to donate a hot coffee to a trucker sitting at -20°C in Ottawa, I could do so from my desk in Austria through a peer-to-peer transaction; Sending bitcoin is like giving someone cash but in digital form.

Confiscation-resistance: bitcoin is also difficult to confiscate. In the example above a Canadian policemen could walk directly to a trucker and even take his phone away. The trucker could theoretically simply borrow his buddy's phone, recreate his wallet using his recovery seed and could immediately recover my donated $5. On a different note, it is not uncommon to sanction nation states by freezing their assets and blocking swift payments. This is usually done on the grounds of terrorism but let me assure you that when there are disagreements and wars, there is never one part which is completely right and another which is completely wrong. What appears to be the fault of a single actor, such a nation state, is often the result of complex power struggles of which we only hear one side of it. Fact is that money is weaponized by freezing monetary reserves, bank accounts and private properties without due process or using partisan legal ways. The point I am trying to make is that it is just much easier to close bank accounts, block credit cards of a political opponent, freeze tangible assets and even monetary reserves such as bonds under the convenient excuse of terrorism and money laundering and without due process, than to confiscate Sats held in private wallets. I also want to make clear that I am not condoning illegal activities of any kind, but I want you to understand that often "illegality" is a blanket word used against opposition as a weapon without due process or with ill-intentioned due legal processes.

What Adolf Hitler did during WWII in Germany or what the South African apartheid regime did was all legal, ...until it wasn't. What the Canadian government did to stump over peaceful civilians demonstrating in Ottawa is all legal under their own emergency act. Instead of legal and illegal, I would rather talk about right and wrong, about freedom and tyranny.

Bitcoin stands for small government, independence, self-reliance, responsibility, freedom, economic fairness and efficiency; Bitcoin will always be a formidable fighter against any form of tyranny because, after all, money is the biggest army.

Financial inclusion: today, about 70% of the world population still has no bank account. These people are excluded by the financial world and will never be able to achieve better standards of living without inclusion. However, most of these people today own a smart phone and have an internet connection, this alone would allow anyone to keep a bitcoin wallet and to become financially included. Going back to El Salvador, I know that Jack Mallers is cooperating with the local government to allow Salvadorians to use Strike® (I have no affiliation with both Mr. Mallers and Strike). With Strike® people in El Salvador may receive funds from their US relatives instantly with extremely low fees and may choose to receive both US dollars or BTC, regardless if the sender sends BTC or US dollars. Now the user in El Salvador may go to the store and buy a Pupusas using just a phone with money generously donated by a family member who is a migrant worker abroad! In a no so distant future that person, who up to today had no bank account, will be able to ask or even offer a loan using the bitcoin's network to financially interact with the world at the speed of light. Financial inclusion, private property rights, censorship-resistance, inconfiscability, the ability to trade and exchange, and privacy are all keys to achieving prosperity, freedom, and happiness.

Security: The bitcoin network is the most secure network in the world as it is protected by an ever-increasing hash rate. As I write this chapter the current network's hash rate is estimated to be 200M TH/s! The more hashing power in the network, the greater its security and its overall resistance to attacks. Just to give you an idea, only 4 years ago the network's hash rate was 13M TH/s. Interestingly even at times of decreasing USD bitcoin valuation, the hash rate tends to increase.

Counterfeit protection: miners confirm every BTC transaction on the network so that you may be sure that the Sats you receive are legitimate.

Cross-Border payments: bitcoin knows no borders. Funds may be transferred from anywhere to anywhere on the planet as cash final transactions.

Information: information and big data is so important that today's most valuable companies are those who are able to collect it and analyze it; Think no further than Google, Facebook, Twitter, Instagram, and Amazon. Those are all digital companies which analyze and monetize information collected from people's interaction. The transition to the information age has not yet really happened with money. Sure, credit card companies and banks collect information through electronic purchases and money movement, but this information is scattered, and settlements still take days to occur. The digitalization of money will improve velocity, commerce and optimize monetary policies. For this purpose, the accuracy and latency (speed) of the data is crucial. Surely central banks are moving towards CBDCs, which will offer many of these advantages, but these are centralized systems which will unfortunately funnel governments to even more overreach and will, without a doubt, further restrict freedom. Bitcoin and the Lightning Network® (no affiliation) will provide extremely precise and transparent data at the speed of light yet safeguarding private ownership, privacy, peer-to-peer exchanges, limited money supply, a truly free market economy and ultimately true freedom.

Bitcoin is not only a better form of money but is THE best form of money ever created. It is not the 21 million coinage limit, the decentralized network or even the proof-of-work protocol alone which make bitcoin great, it is all of bitcoin's core values and its timing of release which make of bitcoin the most important monetary invention ever made.

Bitcoin is the first engineered monetary system built for the benefit of humanity. With bitcoin, inflation, impoverishment, and subservience of the people at the hand of political powers and private interest groups, are just no longer possible. With bitcoin you may save the sweat of your brows for a million years, even forever! With bitcoin you may transfer money (which is work, your work!), through time and space, peer-to-peer; no government or private entity may ever censure it or confiscate it. Bitcoin is work conserved through energy and protected by CPU power as digital monetary private property. Bitcoin is the ultimate form of private property and consequentially of freedom in a digital world.

Bitcoin can neither be replicated or made better through changes to its core values. In fact, a bitcoin replica will have no value as money will flow to the already established network and a change to the bitcoin's protocol which compromises any of its values, will inevitably create yet another hard fork, which is a different coin all together.

Bitcoin does not just fix the two main problems of money today, excessive money supply and governmental overreach, bitcoin allows for a truly modern, digital free market economy which would benefit the whole world.

Chapter three: Freedom and property rights

Like many, I came for the money just to realize that money is time and time is freedom.

Today, I buy, HODL and use bitcoin not only to preserve my wealth, but mostly to protect my very freedom.

As I write this book, in the midst of the Covid-19 pandemic, the word freedom has taken a whole different meaning, it is a word which cannot be taken or used lightly.

Freedom is a born virtue which, historically, humans have heinously mistreated and suppressed. We have the nasty habit of taking freedom away from our own fellow beings as soon as the opportunity presents itself.

Freedom is very hard to achieve, difficult to protect and very easy to lose. Freedom has always come with a very high price tag, a price tag often tinged with blood. Freedom is not, and has never been, free. As a child I grew up in southern Italy in the 1970's and 80's, life seemed simple and good back then, little did I know that the precious (partial and conditional) freedom and wealth I was enjoying was the fruit of defeating Nazi, Fascist and Communist tyrannies, little did I know that that freedom and wellbeing was the fruit of hunger, suffering and more importantly undefiant courage. Now in 2020-2022, as basic rights are treated as privileges and liberties all over the world are under a final tremendous attack, we start to appreciate how precious and costly freedom really is.

But what does it mean to be free? I honestly had to think a little before answering this question as I prepared to write this chapter; The answer is not trivial. This chapter comes on purpose before we discuss the personal wealth effects of adopting bitcoin because freedom is the greater good. Once you understand the real value of bitcoin, you will know that its biggest virtue is its ability to protect liberty and gift us sovereignty.

Freedom, in my opinion, is the ability to choose for oneself without coercion as far as my freedom does not undercut someone else's. Freedom is the ability of expressing our own thoughts and feelings, or freedom of speech. Financially, freedom is the ability to earn money doing something we have passion for, save money in a currency which does not devaluate over time, and spend money in a permissionless and censorship-resistant way.

Surely, we cannot reduce freedom to just financial terms, but without real financial freedom and without strong private property rights, no other freedom may ever be fully obtained.

Freedom to earn my own money: this is the freedom to earn money which truly belongs to me. The government or the bank may restrict, freeze, and even confiscate your funds at any time. Cash or physical gold offer some protection as they may be self custodied, but they may also be easily confiscated. If you live in a western country, do not think that this is something which only happens somewhere else. In Italy, in the 1980's, the government confiscated overnight a portion of all bank deposits to reduce the national debt, in Greece during the 2011 crisis people had restrictions on cash withdrawals. In Italy, again, during the Covid pandemic, people without a vax pass were not allowed to access banks and post offices, making receiving a pension or withdrawing cash extremely difficult if not outright impossible. During the Freedom Convoy-2022 in Canada, as already mentioned, GoFundMe® was forced to freeze donations for over $10 million CAD. Recently PayPal® threatened to freeze funds of people guilty of online hate speech. These are just a few examples on how easily governments and private companies may seize and restrict your own money if held with centralized financial entities. This is also true for crypto if held with centralized exchanges or centralized crypto financial institutions.

However, if you chose self-custody, as I strongly recommend, bitcoin gives you the freedom to earn money which truly belongs to you. Governments may tax profits and hinder bitcoin/FIAT exchanges or ban mining, but no one can ever take Sats away from you or hinder your right and power to dispose of your funds as you freely wish.

Bitcoin is your money! The gene is out of the bottle and there is nothing that can be done to unwind this.

Freedom to save my own money: This is the ability to save the work we perform for future benefit. This freedom is seriously and quickly eroded by inflation, the silent thief. You might take inflation for granted, as a necessary evil, but inflation is a direct result of the monetary supply. If you save in FIAT, you participate into a system where you absolutely have no say on how the monetary supply is managed. The FED and other central banks, decide alone how much money supply they will inject into the system and what interest rates they will apply to your loans and savings. With bitcoin you participate in a system where rules have been written and cannot be changed and where only the free market is at play. There can be a maximum of only 21 million bitcoin, and you know exactly how and when they will be minted. Because of this decentralized system of rules without rulers, you can be sure that the value of your savings will not be diluted by a third party.

The current dollar-dominated FIAT money system is at the end of its debt cycle, for the past 10 years you have not been able to make any interests on your savings as Central Banks have no way of significantly increase the primary interest rate without collapsing the over-leveraged system, any attempts to do so have so far been very short lived. The FIAT money system is nothing more than a house of cards designed to be inflated and collapse to restart just another FIAT cycle! While it does that, your savings are being diluted day after day.

Ironically bitcoin is often accused of being a Ponzi scheme, in reality it is the FIAT money system to be de facto the biggest Ponzi scheme ever created. As we already explained, the FIAT system is built on debt and only works if debt is ever increasing, and if not too many people leave the system at once. It is enough for just a minuscule portion of the population to withdraw their money or a large enough private entity to go insolvent, for the system to fail in a matter of weeks, if not days.

With bitcoin you can now save again in a digital asset protected by an incredible amount of CPU power and energy, limited supply and which may be transferred frictionless at the speed of light anytime and anywhere.

Freedom to spend my own money: This is the freedom to spend, or use, your money as you wish. This freedom is granted partially and conditionally by the current FIAT system and these conditions have become very clear during the Covid pandemic. You can go to the grocery store and buy some food and drinks and pay with cash or a with credit card, unless you do not comply to governments' regulations. People who opposed mandatory inoculation usually have something in common, they oppose government overreach and value individual freedoms. This allows governments and the press to quickly stamp these individuals as right extremists, conspiracy theorists and anti-vaxers, all undemocratic vilifying pejoratives to dismiss dissent and avoid discourse. People who do not respond to persuasion and do not comply to coercion oppose the common good, they need to be repressed and ostracized as they are a true danger to the power structure. Therefore, during the Covid pandemic opponents were first locked into their homes, then allowed to just purchase basic goods, and finally banned from working in a wicked but at the same time desperate attempt to marginalize and coerce. Once CBDCs come into play, unless the free people of the world can steer away from this Coup d'état which also foresees the elimination of cash, people will have even less options but to comply. In such a totalitarian control system, camouflaged by good words such as "the common benefit" and "inclusion" but tyrannical at its root as it does not allow for dissent and does not allow for freedom of choice, the only way you would be allowed to freely own and spend your own money would be through bitcoin, or any non-government controlled cryptocurrency; However, I specifically refer to bitcoin as in my personal opinion it is the most liquid, decentralized and secured cryptocurrency with intrinsic value and a limited supply which may be transferred peer-to-peer at the speed of light.

This is the reality we all face, we get paid in a currency which we not necessarily wish and which we cannot really control, we lose a tremendous amount of purchasing power to inflation and no interest-bearing saving accounts, and we cannot necessarily use our money when and how we wish!

Ironically and sadly, these processes which deeply erode fundamental freedoms happen with the acquiescence of the very people whose freedoms are being taken away. This has been achieved through a long and systematic erosion process which has slowly chipped away freedom and notions of freedom through the educational system, mainstream media, TV shows, movies and the usual crisis used to scare people into subservience in exchange of "public safety" and "the common good". The road to hell is paved by nice intentions, and so is the road to total control and tyranny.

Nice intentions muffled by "the common good", "the common safety", "the common health" and "the politically correct". I thought we went down this pathway before in history through a multitude of fascist, communist and socialist revolutions and it never worked out that well!

The best way to the common good is to safeguard individual freedoms. This has been the bedrock of the American experiment as documented in the American Constitution and Bill of Rights. Individual rights have allowed free enterprise to prosper, have allowed small and medium businesses to flourish giving wealth and independence to millions of families. As individual rights are respected, equal opportunities arise, a free-market economy is allowed to flourish and the common good is maximized. If we allow politicians, governmental, non-governmental organizations, and multinational companies to decide what is right and wrong for the common good, we slip very quickly and without exceptions into tyranny and into unhappiness. It is an illusion that people should have equal outcomes, it is an illusion to think that a small group of people may rightfully decide what is good for everyone else. If you have never read Adam Smith's book, The Wealth of Nations, please do so. It will teach you that individual sovereignty, specialization, and trade are the secret to wealth and the true common good. A central decisional and economic system has never and will never work, no matter how sophisticated the system is and how well-spoken its proponents are.

We now live in times where people get unjustly taxed. An individual making $100.000 a year may easily pay 50% in direct taxation, mandatory pension funds and mandatory health care participation funds (this is true in some US states and most European Nations). Furthermore, at least in Europe, people pay about 20% sales tax and about 70% taxes at the pump, without counting the occasional additional governmental contribution paid as parking and speeding tickets. For many of us, counting direct and indirect taxation, we work from January 1st to mid-September for the government; add inflation, which is hidden taxation, taxes on real estate sales and, as a final insult to injury, inheritance taxes once you die to the final bill, and you realize that you are nothing else than a slave, a living being born and built to work for someone else. This level of taxation and monetary control gives asymmetric power to the government and takes disproportionate economic power away from the private citizen.

Politically, we not only have elected officials making laws and regulations, but we have powerful unelected national and international organizations, health organizations, economic forums etc., which are able to forcefully influence laws and regulations without direct accountability. Moreover, during the past decades, small and medium businesses have often gone out of business or have been merged into large multinational organizations. The national political power, coupled with unelected national and international organizations through partnerships with large multinational corporations employing millions of people, a captured press and an ideologically driven judicial systems have slowly but surely eroded most individual freedoms.

Sadly, the true value of freedom, independence and self-reliance are no longer thought in schools, and most people do not even realize that they are not free. We, in the western world, live in democratic and free nations which are really so only on paper. In reality, we are merely allowed to live with very limited self-decisional powers which become smaller and smaller with every year which passes by. We live in a true matrix which is fine for most people as long as there is enough food, heating in winter, the possibility to lease a car and afford the occasional vacation. As long as most people are allowed to have this, they will never realize that they have no freedom and will never protest even if the most essential freedoms are taken away. We have seen it during the covid pandemic, only a small percentage of people protested the loss of bodily autonomy, freedom of speech, freedom to assemble, freedom to choose how we are governed, freedom to earn, save and spend our own money. Most people either complained but complied, or happily complied.

We are unfortunately nothing more than human cattle, we stay in our fenced green pasture because our primary needs are taken care of, but we do not see that we are free within a prison and, sadly, we do not realize that we have the strength to walk out of our fence at any time.

I would like to spend now a few more words on CBDCs, or FIAT digital currencies, as already mentioned. CBDCs will most likely be paid directly to you by your Central Bank without the local private bank as an intermediary. Most notably digital currencies will be programmable and 100% trackable. What that means is that the central bank has the full power to decide the interest rate (or negative interest rate) you get, where, when, and on what you may spend your money, and has even the power to freeze your ability to earn and use your money by mouse click, or worse using artificial intelligence with decision-making powers. While they offer many undeniable practical benefits to the end user (the citizen), these benefits are just a carrot. CBDCs have been built to solely facilitate governments' objectives, eliminate peer-to-peer cash payments, and will become an incredible weapon of mass control in the hands of nefarious actors once coupled with digital IDs, face recognition, and internet-use restrictions. What a temptation! Do you really think that governments will not use this technology to expand even further their power and control? And once governments have such a power, do you think they will freely relinquish it? Think again!!

Bitcoin is also digital money, but the key difference with CBDCs is that bitcoin is decentralized, is built on a proof-of-work protocol which secures its integrity, has a known fixed supply, is censorship resistance, is unconfiscatable, is backed by CPU power and energy, and allows for peer-to-peer transactions which are cash final.

Bitcoin is in one word Sovereign!

CBDCs, by contrast, offer none of that! I have often heard that once CBDCs are rolled out, bitcoin has no reason to exist. This is however blatantly and ignorantly false; bitcoin is at the exact antipode of CBDCs. One stands for individual freedoms, the other stands for governmental overpower.

Knowing how "democratic" and "free" countries such as Australia, New Zeeland the EU, Canada and even to a certain extend most of the U.S. behaved during the Covid pandemic, bitcoin is truly a gift; Once CBDCs are rolled out, the only way to deter total control systems are decentralized independent monetary systems.

As I mentioned already before, freedom is the greater good, it is hard and costly to preserve, and relatively easy to underestimate and lose.

Freedom is strictly connected to the protection of individual rights, property rights, decentralization of powers and the ability to perform peer-to-peer transactions.

"You will own nothing, and you will be happy", you know exactly which direction the world will take if such dystopian philosophy is allowed to be adopted and cemented in our society.

Property rights, decentralization and monetary freedom are the underlying principles of personal freedoms and are necessary for real wealth creation and wide distribution. You just cannot have personal freedoms without monetary freedom and because money represent the fruits of your labor, if you cannot own and control your own money, you really are not allowed to own and control anything.

Bitcoin is just that: the ultimate private property kept in cyberspace protected by energy and CPU power through a decentralized net of miners, nodes, and users! it allows you to take full and complete ownership - although with this privilege comes responsibility - of your financial assets through the use of digitally created decentralized hard money.

Freedom, ownership, and decentralization are the ingredients of a free market economy, which is the only system that has proven to work in creating real and widespread wealth and happiness. There can be no real free-market economy without strong property rights laws and can be no real freedom without true decentralization of powers. This is exactly what bitcoin gives you, the ability to earn, own and spend your own money and a decentralized network with the same rules for everyone. Bitcoin represents, therefore, the very essence of decentralization of powers, property rights, free market capitalism and free societies.

Bitcoin is a beacon of freedom for the people and will create, once adopted, true long-lasting sustainable wealth and peace for the whole planet. Many say that since the US dollar is no longer backed by gold, it is backed by war. There is for sure a lot of truth behind this sentence if you just think about the unlimited U.S. military budget granted by the FIAT money system and its use of military force around the world.

Bitcoin cannot allow unlimited military budgets by definition and might well be one of the main factors, if not the main one, for world peace.

Centralization of power has always been the greatest temptation of the ruling class. The most extreme forms of centralization can be found in countries where power is held by one person without a true independent counterweight and maintained through violence. Think about the communist Soviet Union, or of countries such as North Korea and Iran; These are countries which strongly advocate and use centralized power, centralized economic planning, party press and dissidents' repression to rule. The problem with these models is that they only created widespread poverty which in the long term cause people to revolt.

The United States, as it was founded, constituted the complete opposite. Truly separate branches of government, a small federal government, free banking, independent federal states, local and federal police, federal and state armed forces and a free press. All this has created without a doubt the freest, wealthiest and the most powerful nation on earth. However, all this has been heavily eroded with time. In today's technologically advanced world, concentration of power and old-fashioned tyranny is unfolding again but in a much more sophisticated and camouflaged way. The prime example is China. Power is concentrated within the communist party, yet enterprises are allowed to flourish as long as they ally with the central government. This alliance, between private enterprises and central government, the alignment of the educational system, media and all branches of government, coupled with tools such as the social credit score and digital control systems, has created an outstanding economic engine, a decent middle class yet a freedom-less society.

The United States has seen similar shifts characterized by the creation of large central banks, concentration of powers, an ideological and political alignment of the executive, legislative and judiciary branches, an ideologically aligned legacy media (with few exceptions), a controlled big tech, the ideologization of at least part of the military, the weaponization of the FBI and the CIA and the infiltration and capture of governmental health agencies. This alignment is not perfect and as strong as in China, states still hold much power to counterweight the central federal government, and not all companies are ideologically aligned, yet today's United States of America is far, far away from the decentralized free nation it was just a century ago. I actually believe that the true free days of the United States ended with the assassination of JFK.

This centralization process does not allow for true freedom to flourish and is a very refined system as it allows its citizens to stay out of poverty (to avoid revolts) yet keeps most of the population caged in a hamster wheel through the weaponization of the educational system, the information channels and of course the FIAT money system.

Interestingly private forums have been advocating and actively implementing the alliance between international bodies, governments, large corporations, media, and big-tech in a fashion which resembles a technologically advanced and a modern version of the communist and fascist party. Many think that the fascist and communist parties were at the antipodes, but this is not true. Both were authoritarian dictatorships which destroyed individual freedoms for the common social good, both were evil socialistic ideologies.

This is a very dangerous development as on paper democracy and decentralization of powers still exist but in reality, all powers move at unison through private and public partnerships aided by advanced technological societal control.

One of the ways used to bring the private sector under compliance is the ESG system (environmental social governance). Under ESG, environmental sustainability has been used to force compliance by limiting access to credit. This is a way to force the private sector to move in unison with public interests, which are now agreed and coordinated in private international forums. It is very interesting, for example, to notice how most of these companies have almost without exception adopted Covid-19 vaccinations as a pre-requisite for employment, even as we know that these gene-therapies never stop transmission of the virus.

As you can see, as small businesses have been pushed to extinction forcing most people to work for large, aligned organizations; as democracy allows choices of the same things in just slightly different flavors, there is no much real freedom in the western world left today. Interestingly, during the Covid-19 pandemic, large businesses were quickly declared essentials and allowed to operate, while small businesses were forced to shut down. Shutting down independent small sources of income, reduces any chance to independent free choice to almost zero.

Sadly, most of the population does not realize all this.

Centralization has always and will always be the opposite of freedom.

As a pure decentralized monetary network, bitcoin is the most powerful tool for individual and collective freedom and peace. It does not matter what governments do, people have now the freedom to choose how and when to interact economically with each other at the speed of light without borders and without any third-party, yet with full trust.

Bitcoin is pure economic decentralization and is therefore not only the most powerful vector and protector of freedom, but it has the potential to stop wars and exploitation, to promote widespread peace and freedom.

This revolution against tyranny can be fought and won without a bullet being fired, without any shedding of blood.

All is needed is for people to adopt bitcoin.

Chapter four: Chancellor on the brink of second bailout for banks

On January 3rd, 2009, the first event on the bitcoin blockchain occurred. The first bitcoin block, or The Genesis Block, contained a phrase:

"Chancellor on brink of second bailout for banks"

The world changed forever......

While the white paper describes what (on the surface) is a simple system for electronic peer-to-peer payments, the phrase contained in the genesis block and the historical time frame of the great financial crisis of 2008/2009, left no doubt that bitcoin was not only an e-cash payment system, but was meant to threaten and replace the very core of an unfair financial system, a system which privileges the minority at the expense of the working majority, a system which promotes injustice, inequality, and wars. A system which promotes financial captivity.,

The 2008/2009 financial crisis, fueled by the sub-prime loans showed in all its power how fragile and unfair the world financial organizations were. Millions were left unemployed; many lost their homes, while big banks and big businesses got bailed-out with trillions of freshly minted dollars. Profits were privatized but losses were socialized as bailouts were solely paid by taxpayers. Some financial institutions even used the dollars they received from the bailouts to buy foreclosed homes at much discounted prices, a disgusting takeover of private property with fake printed money by large financiers. Proponents of the great government intervention say that it was a necessary evil to avoid mass unemployment and a second great depression, or for the "common good.

Critics say that the printing press benefited only Wall Street, bankers and politicians, who are the ones which created the crisis in the first place, while robbed the working savers and distorted the free-market economy, which was in desperate need of a downturn and a healthy reset. The 2008-crisis bailouts allowed the sick elements of the economy to survive to the detriment of a healthy market economy. The "free American economy" was not that free after all, the free market mechanism of survival of the fittest was not allowed to work, the invisible hand which Adam Smith wrote about in "the wealth of nations" was not allowed to do its job. We might have avoided short term pain, but we were left with ever bigger governments, over-powerful multinationals, and a mountain of common debt to the detriment of future generations.

Was bitcoin's unleash during the peak of the great financial crisis intentional or just a fortunate coincidence? I tend to believe that bitcoin was programmed in the years prior to 2008. People who followed closely in which direction we had been going for decades, knew already that the day of reckon would eventually come and that personal financial freedom was being eroded at an ever-increasing speed. The genesis block is for me proof that bitcoin's release during the great financial crisis was indeed intentional.

Satoshi built the foundation of a libertarian financial system based on rules without rulers, fairness, and decentralized trust.

We do not know who Satoshi is (or was), but we know that 12 years after the Genesis Block, bitcoin is still there and is continuously growing in numbers of users, value, security, and usability. A new digital financial system has emerged and will conquer the world. The interesting part is that Satoshi did not do it for its own financial interest (at least as of now) as all the 1 million bitcoin he mined are still there unmoved, although they are now worth billions of US dollars. Satoshi left humanity with an incredible gift which will enable us to unchain from the unjust governance of central banks, which are nothing else than banking cartels at the service of powerful elites.

Let's be clear, "Chancellor on brink of second bailout for banks" is a strong political statement, a declaration of war. The gene was let out of the bottle, released to destroy fake and corrupt money and to replace it with real sound digital money for the benefit of humanity. The war will not be won without a hard fight because at the very core of power is monetary control, you will see government-bans as they try to defend their currencies from the alpha predator, un-bans as countries try to regain strategical advantages, secret acquisitions of bitcoin while at the same time telling people that bitcoin is the ultimate evil; but at the end, ultimate strength will prevail!

it cannot be any other way; Darwin was and will always be right.

Chapter five: I came for the money, but I stayed for freedom, as money is time and time is freedom.

Somehow, I was wired for freedom and independence since birth, maybe you feel the same way and that is a reason why you decided to buy this book. There are some instances of my life's history which are indelibly engraved in my memory. When I was a young teen, I started getting bullied. My parents made me changed high school, but things got worse instead of better; At one point I started skipping school, sometimes I would ride the same bus 5-6 hours a day just to avoid getting ridiculed and shoved by my classmates. I lost every interest in education, my grades changed from great to horrible. This loneliness motivated me to look for something different, a better place, a new experience. I searched for schools in the United States looking for more opportunities. The search was not easy back then without the internet, if I actually think about it, how could have it been even possible without the internet? I remember writing letters back and forth, waiting for weeks to get any response and calling from extremely expensive phone booths trying to get information using my broken English. At the age of 16, during my junior high-school year I applied to attend Brigham Young University. I met an American Mormon missionary who helped me through the application and tuition seemed affordable in comparison to other universities, furthermore I was told I could have worked part time to help with the expenses. A crazy dream as I did not come from a wealthy family, in fact quite the opposite. Not because my family was poor, my father worked for the government as a work compensation insurance agent and would work evenings as an accountant for a construction company, my mother was a kindergarten teacher. In southern Italy we were middle class, but nothing compared to the American middle class, our wages were much lower, our apartments much smaller, are cars much humbler. US education was only possible at that time, but probably this is just as true today, for very rich people. I naively hoped to be able to live in the land of the free which I envisioned through movies such as "The Karate Kid", make new friends, work part time, and play sports. All this was not possible in southern Italy. The application process was made tedious by language barriers, a slow mailing process, bank statements requirements necessary to show that my family had enough funds to support me (which they didn't) and an English test which I had to pass. I remember that we got all the documentation required and all I needed to be able to start school was passing an English language proficiency test (TOEFL) with a score of at least 500. I had been studying English for years in school, but my language skills were not proficient. I bought TOEFL prep-books, and I studied every day for months to prepare for this test. My first attempt was at the American military base of Sigonella, Sicily. I took a train for the first time in my life, and I traveled alone all night. In Sicily, I slept one night with friends of friends who were very nice to me, they even drove me to the base to take the test. After the test, I traveled back and waited patiently for weeks to get the test results back. I do not remember the score, but it was far below 500. I felt down, terrible, depressed. I was getting bad grades at school and the failed TOEFL test confirmed that I just was not smart enough. There was another chance to retake the test in Rome a few months later, so I started studying for it again. My cousin Antonello drove me there, I took the test and again waited weeks for the test results to come back: 489..., again short of 500 by just a few points. I went home and cried in my room, I took the application and threw it out of the door. My mother picked it up and calmed me down, there will be a way she said. We called in the U.S. again and the administration told me that there was, within the university, an English school for foreigners; I applied, and I was accepted knowing I only had enough money to stay there for a semester. In fact, students attending the English learning center were not allowed to work but I needed a part time job to have the means to study there. I had one shot, I took it! There I was, the first Italian ever to attend that school, I studied a lot and after a semester I took the TOEFL and got a score of well over 600! After a two-years application process, I finally succeeded and I was admitted to Brigham Young

University in Provo, Utah. It was fun and tough at the same time. For the first two years I was not able to fly back home, tickets were just too expensive. I worked 20 hours a week during regular semesters and full-time during summers while taking only one tennis class to keep enrollment. It was tough, but such a great experience!

There in the U.S. I learned the meaning of freedom by studying the American Constitution, the Bill of Rights and by living the "American way of life". I remember trips through the Utah and Nevada deserts on a used Honda 500 motorcycle with no helmet, a pair of sunglasses, a leather jacket, a tent, and 100 dollars in my pocket to last me 2 weeks in gas and food. I also remember stupid little things like wearing shorts in the middle of the Utah winter just to be cool… or going to the grocery store wearing my pajamas without anyone caring…things which were all unthinkable in Italy. I had the freedom to do whatever I wanted as long as I did not hurt anybody else, yet the rule of law was strong and present. People drove respectfully of each other; car thefts were extremely rare, and people often left their homes open even at night. Those little things, so much different from my southern Italian culture, taught me a lot about being and feeling free. Those were wonderful years whose memories I still deeply cherish. Those terrible high school years did serve their purpose, first they made me stronger and secondly, they gave me the chance to look for other opportunities which opened many new doors. I learned English, earned a degree in business, had an incredible amount of fun, and tasted real freedom.

After finishing my first degree at Brigham Young in 1997, I went back to Italy. I came back home with my backpack full of knowledge and dreams, I had the desire to make it in the real world. The greatest lesson I brought back from Utah was that freedom, independence, individual liberties, and self-reliance are the greater goods. Back in Italy I landed my first job with a retail chain and then with a pharmaceutical company. As I prepared to start employment, I remember going to the HR office and I was asked for my bank account where they could wire my monthly salary, a meager $1200 a month. I told the HR worker I did not have or want a bank account as it would have cost me $25 in monthly fees. In the US my bank account used to be for free! I tried asking for a check, but I quickly figured out that I could not cash a check without a bank account, in fact I could not even pay my utilities without a bank account. I then asked tenaciously for a cash payment, but that was not a viable option. Why was I being forced to have a bank account that cost me 2% of my monthly salary, I naively asked myself? As you can imagine I finally gave in and opened the (damn) bank account, as I really had no other option.

In 1998 I visited my parents in Puglia, southern Italy. While there I wanted to buy something for which I needed 10 million Liras (about USD 5.000). I had sufficient funds in my account but as I could not withdraw so much money from the ATM I went inside the local branch and asked to withdraw what I needed, the bank director came and asked me why I needed the money, my reply was that it was none of his business. No, he replied, you need to go to your home branch and ask the bank director there in advance, you cannot just come into a bank and request so much money at once! This was for me a great weak up call;... I could not believe it! I did not have access to my money how and when I needed it.

I told you this little story just to show you the independent free spirit I always had. I wanted to do my part for society as a law-abiding citizen, but at the same time I always had that renegade spirit in me which constantly thrives for truth, justice, independence, and freedom.

A famous philosopher said: "I think therefore I am", I like to say: "I can choose therefore I am". I am sure a lot of you feel the same and that is the reason you were probably attracted by this book, the simple desire for financial independence and freedom.

In the US, as I mentioned, I was able to attend a prestigious Business School for about 5 years, yet I really do not remember that someone ever taught me that FIAT money is created as debt and can only function if more debt is created. Nobody ever taught me that the Federal Reserve System is a private cartel organized secretly at Jekyll Island who took the monopoly of printing and issuing legal tender, the greatest power a nation can have. I also do not remember being taught the principle of asset accumulation for the purpose of creating long term wealth. I was thought and encouraged to save, to pay off my mortgage early, to work as a diligent "soldier", but never to buy real assets and gain financial freedom and independence.

Let's now move forward to April 2020, at the time I was 46 years old, 24 years after graduating from Brigham Young. I started thinking that most likely I already lived more than half of my life. Three months later I was scheduled to marry the love of my life, my second and hopefully last marriage. We both had a previous marriage gone bad and together we had 5 children. Federica, our only common child, was only 4 months old. I had 3 children from my disastrous first marriage, Tina had a child from her first. We decided to treat each child as our own and to go through the journey of our life together never regretting our past but cheering the fact that hardships made us stronger, and that hardships made us find each other.

On 04th July, 2020, (what a significant date which came absolutely by chance) we were supposed to hike to a small church in the mountains, and there promise each other to walk the rest of our lives together.

We planned to have a simple, meaningful wedding. Only strict family members and just a couple of childhood friends were going to be invited. I was going to need 7,000 Euros to cover for the wedding expenses.

I looked at my bank account and it showed a balance just over EUR 7,000.

No problem I thought, I will use the 7.000 for the wedding and I will build our finances back up, I will save money again.

At the time, I really did not want to think about money, but in the back of my mind I have always wanted to achieve some sort of economic security and financial independence. I just wanted to be happy, after all, love and happiness are what we live for and have always been for me a priority; However, my mind started to think and wonder about how I could be so poor? Surely the first marriage hit my finances hard, but I worked my whole life and so did my (soon to be) wife. We either smoked nor drink, we did not gamble, our cars were just average, and so were our clothes. Where did the money go?

Why am I just a step away from a financial disaster? how could I ever survive illness or unemployment? How could I ever retire?

I never really sought great riches, but at the very least I always wanted to live my life feeling somewhat financially secure! After 7 total years of college (after Brigham Young I took a second degree in nursing) and 20 years of work I should have reached some sort of financial security! How did I find myself in this dire situation? I always thought of myself as an intelligent guy and a good saver, how stupid I really am in managing my finances? Because if at 46 all I could count on is two old cars, 25 years left to pay on my mortgage and 7.000 bucks in my bank account...., well something must be really, really wrong!

As I started thinking about my past in the search for wisdom, my thoughts went back to 2008. Back then, I had just graduated from nursing school (my second degree), and I was able to find employment as a Registered Nurse in the cardiac ICU at the Florida University Hospital (go Gators!). I remember that that year the financial world came crashing down, banks and big businesses got bailed out while millions of people lost everything including their homes. I was glued to the TV, I will never forget the images of people losing everything being projected around the clock by all news outlets. I had the childhood dream of owning my own house, a 3 bedrooms single-family-home with a garage and a yard. I remember that working in the ICU I was being paid $ 20 / hr. for regular time, $ 30 dollars / hr. for overtime. Holidays were paid double, so I worked every single holiday!

The first year as a Registered Nurse, I sacrificed everything by working an average of 72 hours a week in order to save for a house down payment. It was real hard work, I had to be extremely careful with the medications I gave; Most of my patients were intubated and fighting for their lives, they depended on me doing a good job to stay alive. I remember that after my shift, on the way home, I often pulled over and slept for an hour as I was just too tired to keep on driving. Once at home, during the day I was only able to sleep a total of 4 to 6 hours, I was just not a day sleeper! Giving it all that I had and sacrificing time with my kids and even my health, I proudly saved $ 50.000 that year. I felt good about myself. As a married student, just a year earlier, I used to survive on 500 dollars a month, my lunch used to be roman noodles with a peanut butter & jelly sandwich as desert, now I was able to afford better groceries and even save for my dream, for my own house. In 2010 I bought a lot and finally hired a contractor. My Budget was $500.000, which in the area where I lived would have bought me an average home. As the house was being built, construction costs skyrocketed to $600.000. To make ends meet I tiled all floors myself (after work and on days off) and I painted all inner and outer walls. Today I realize that I was saving like a mad man, I was working as hard as I possibly could, but by the time I saved the 50.000 dollars needed for the down payment, housing cost increased by 100.000 dollars. I kept my head down and worked, but the system was rigged against me. I was running on a treadmill like crazy just to get nowhere!

In 2008 the FED printed huge amounts of money to save the banks and big businesses from going under. At the end of the day the financial collapse was the fruit of greed, corruption, and bad monetary policies, but the bills got paid by the working classes. A huge wealth transfer happened from the working class to the top 1%. In fact, in my own experience, my savings got diluted as the FED printed money a lot faster than I was ever able to put aside. The worse part was that I had no say in it!

Now I know how things worked during the 2008-2009 financial crisis...,banks created the problem by lending money to pretty much anyone through the so-called subprime loans, then they would re-package the loans (knowing that a lot of them were very high risk) and got rid of the liabilities by selling them to Wall Street, who would then market them as "safe" mortgage-backed securities for higher yields. By doing so banks profited immensely and at the same time inflated the housing market through the creation of trillions in freshly minted money, or new debt. When the system collapsed, triggered by the fall of Lehman Brothers, instead of having the corrupt go to jail, banks were bailed out through government aid (new debt again) while many private citizens lost everything.

These guys truly robbed us blind; First they diluted our savings through asset inflation and now are even buying our foreclosed properties dirt cheap using freshly printed monopoly money.

Profits were privatized but losses were socialized!

Now, as I write this book in 2021-2022, the situation has not changed much since 2008. The cause is different, a pandemic this time, but the underlying issue is the same. The system is built on a debt-generated money supply, and the government is supporting all big businesses by printing money out of thin air just to keep the house of card from collapsing. Big businesses, banks, and Wall Street are just not allowed to fail. The market economy, the invisible hand described by Adam Smith in his famous book "The Wealth of Nations", is not allowed to work and has not been allowed to work for a very long time.

Did you really think that you, in the United States of America, live in a truly free capitalistic country? Please wake up! Americans today live in a socialistic market economy which is always mores socialistic and always less capitalistic. The only way to keep it afloat is by enforcing more and more central control measures with the assent of the majority of the public who have become unaware of what is really going on, numbed through the educational system, the media, and big-tech.

And here they came, mandatory inoculations, digital IDs and a looming social credit scores with CBDCs just a couple of years away from implementation.

Will we soon own nothing and be happy? most likely this is the way it is going to be unless the public opinion is able to shift, unless we are able to steer the world again towards true freedom and true market economies.

Save big banks and corporations, make the working-class dependent on large corporations and social measures, introduce behavioral control through mass manipulation, and abolish freedom of speech by declaring all dissonating voices misinformation, terrorism and hate speech. Adopt a social credit score, top it all up with CBDCs for total control and surveillance and lack of monetary ownership, take private property away through inflation, taxation, and impoverishment of the middle class, adopt artificial intelligence and we might soon have a world which will resemble China on steroids, a real nightmare! A world in which I, quite frankly, would not want to live in.

Is this what the pandemic was all about? A catalyst to realize "The fourth industrial revolution" through the big financial reset needed to fix the house of cards built on debt, wars, and exploitation during the past 100 years? A useful catalyst to bring humanity under total control?

The true capitalist world Adam Smith described in his book, allowed for the market, the invisible hand, to rebalance the economy. Specialization and trade would allow wealth creation and benefit everyone, just as a rising sea lifts all boats. As governments get larger by the day and their interventions do not allow big businesses, banks, and Wall Street to go bust, the invisible hand is no longer able to work and keep things in a healthy balance. In fact, the role of economic corrections (downturns), is necessary to wipe out any weak points and inefficiencies for the benefit of a healthy balanced economy which in return builds a healthy and wealthy society. An economy where so many things are too big to fail, is really a socialistic-oligarchic-capital economy based on power concentration and sustained by money printing and social control. A house of card ready to fall and crumble, and it would fall and crumble as soon as the markets are allowed to freely act. Right now, only a minority of big business and very wealthy individuals, have mostly access to this artificially created cheap capital used for assets accumulation. This process inflates assets' prices and makes owners richer and hard-working people poorer by diluting their savings at an ever-increasing speed. The system is only kept from crumbling by concentrating more and more powers into the hands of our masters and by forcing the rest of us to give up our freedoms and wealth in the name of alleged money laundering, child sex trafficking and the environment. All this has happened because of debt-money creation: FIAT money.

I now realize that as I saved for that first house of mine, we were being robbed in plain sight as central banks diluted our savings without our permission and favored the few at the expense of the many, the savers.

If we really think about it, we (the working class) pay income taxes (big businesses do not, or do so only marginally), we pay value added taxes (businesses do not), and the little that we are able to save is taken away from the silent thief of inflation just because central banks decide to print a disproportionate amount of money! At least in the past we used to get some interest from our savings' account, but interests on savings are today only a far-gone memory. The system is rigged, and unless we learn how to outsmart our masters, or rebuild the system, we are going to remain poor and subservient for the rest of our life, we are going to remain captive like a hamster running in a wheel with the illusion of reaching the unattainable goal of economic freedom.

Most of us are prisoners, slaves without chains to the system, without any hope and with the illusion of being free.

I started asking myself questions, how can I change this? What can I do to pay off my mortgage and gain a sense of security and independence? What can I do to earn my freedom?

I started doing some research looking for wisdom and knowledge, interestingly I found out that one of the best place to learn nowadays is YouTube (and the likes) as long as you try to pick reputable sources.

Searching I found interviews with Max Keiser, Robert Kiyosaki, Anthony Pompliano, Michael Saylor, Raoul Pal, Andreas Antonopoulos, Simon Dixon, Peter McCormack, Benjamin Owen...(I have no affiliation with any of these people) just to name a few. I also read "Rich Dad Poor Dad®" by Robert Kiyosaki, and I understood that to become free I first had to understand what real money and real assets are, I needed to start accumulating them, I needed to stop working for money and start having money work for me. Robert's book cost me $10 and in retrospect it helped me more than the 4 years and the $100.000 spent in Business School. If you read this, thank you Robert Kyosaki, you have been a great teacher.

I took out an excel table and I figured out much money I was left over with at the end of the month after paying all my expenses. Instead of saving it, I now needed to invest it and buy assets as Robert Kiyosaki taught. I was really the poor dad in his book, and I did not want to die as a poor dad. But what assets can I buy starting from scratch and with only a few hundred dollars' worth of monthly residual income?

I had no money to buy rental property, I thought, but I can start buying some stocks, which I did. A few months later I bought my first 1-oz of gold, real money. Then I came across a YouTube video interview between Robert Kiyosaki and Anthony Pompliano where they talked about bitcoin...

What, bitcoin? That is definitely not a hard asset! A crypto currency which you can just mine off your PC? I actually wanted to start mining bitcoin in 2009 from my dorm room in college, I must have been one of the first in the world to register, but my laptop was a piece of junk and it seemed technically too difficult for me at the time. I let mining bitcoin go, also because I did not want to take time away from studying and lower my 3.94 gpa....in retrospect, a very bad decision!

I then came across bitcoin again in 2016-2017 when it crashed from $20.000 to $7.000 with the mainstream news announcing this epic crash widely to protect naive citizens from falling victim of this high-tech scam. After watching Pompliano's video, however, I became very curious about bitcoin, so I tried to get some information from a trusted sources by asking my bank director about it:

"It is a scam, money for drug dealers and pedophiles" he told me, " lots of my clients have lost lots of money in it".

I quickly decided that I did not want anything to do with it. However, a few months later I rewatched the same YouTube video, which you may also view for your enjoyment: https://www.youtube.com/watch?v=c-G99P0K_r4

Those guys on YouTube were talking about bitcoin in a much different way than my bank director. I decided that I needed to spend some serious time researching about it If I really wanted to understand it. The more I read, the more videos I watched, the more I started to realize that there was much more than met the eye. I went into a rabbit hole as I just had to learn more and more about it.

I spent literally hundreds of hours researching bitcoin, which then brought me to learn more about the crypto industry as a whole. I realized that Crypto, or blockchain technologies in general, is the future. I realized we were living a revolution bigger than the one experienced in the 90's with the rise of the internet. Blockchain technologies will change forever how we transact with each other and how data is kept and distributed, it will change forever how we save and invest money, it will change forever as we see and understand property rights. Only bitcoin can give back freedom and dignity to humanity, and this is by no means an overstatement.

As I started researching bitcoin, I learned how to buy it from reputable sources and how to safely store it. With a leap of faith, something which did not came from my intellectual understanding but as an instinct within me (it was sincerely almost like a spiritual experience), I placed slowly some of my monthly savings into bitcoin (no financial advice, investing in bitcoin is extremely risky and investing a large quantity of own wealth in one risky investment is never recommended). I guess my instinct was right as I started accumulating Sats just before the 2020-2021 bull market. I literally struggled financially my whole life, I have always worried about making ends meet and providing for my children. For the first time in my life, I felt I was going to be ok. I saw my wealth grow very rapidly and the more I researched the more I learned that bitcoin can literally make me free.

With bitcoin, I can save again and keep the value of my savings and even significantly increase my wealth. With bitcoin I own my money and I can save it or spend it as I wish. Bitcoin is much more than wealth creation for private citizens, nation states can now grow debt free and prosperous for the benefit of their own citizens. It will not be long until bitcoin will be held as treasury reserve by many nation states lead by visionary leaders, leaders who understand that by holding bitcoin they will free their countries from the debt trap webbed by the international monetary powers who present themselves as savers when in reality, they are the very ones who keep poor nations enslaved aided by corrupt local politicians. These nations can now gain international economic and political strength for the benefit of their own citizens. This is a revolution poised to happen, and while it is mostly citizens of the "first" world who initially adopted bitcoin to increase their wealth, it's the developing nations who will be the first to unchain themselves from financial slavery and neo colonialism by adopting bitcoin.

My bank director was wrong, not because he was intentionally trying to damage me, but because he could only see the narrative fed to him by his organization and because, quite frankly, he did not invest the time in trying to understand what bitcoin and blockchain cryptography really are.

No pain no gain, this is true in all aspects of life. You must be willing to take the time to understand, and you need to be willing to have skin in the game to succeed.

This book is a journey, I will teach you what I have learned and hopefully you will keep learning beyond this book. The traditional educational system has failed, or in actuality is intentionally built to keep you in the matrix. Once you understand what is really going on behind the smoke screen, with bitcoin you have an incredibly powerful tool and ally to free yourself through real sound digital money, digital gold, which you may own, save, and spend.

If you use this knowledge wisely, if you stay humble, bitcoin will change your life (and that of your children) for the better.... at least financially.

As I stated, I came for the money as I was attracted by the huge FIAT gains bitcoin offers, but I stayed for freedom as I understood that holding a digital asset which I may really own without the need of a third party and which I may spend digitally through peer-to-peer transactions is freedom. Owning a digital scarce asset which generally appreciates in value, although affected by huge short-term speculative fluctuations, allows me to save the sweat of my brows for future benefits without having to be diluted by the printing press. With bitcoin I can transfer my money, for which I worked hard and for which I already paid lots of taxes, anytime and anywhere in the world without having to ask permission to do so, without having to justify where and how I got that money, without being stopped at airports and be put on watch-lists for no reasons. Governments can take away what you earn through direct and indirect taxation, governments can freeze your bank accounts in a heartbeat if they do not like you, government may stop you from transferring funds across borders, governments will take the little you are left with once you are dead through succession taxes. With bitcoin you are your own government, you are financially sovereign, you are financially free and once you are financially free you can consider yourself a free man! You can do with your time whatever you want, you can work the job you are the most passionate about, you can enjoy life on earth!

Even in this incredibly perilous time when everything seems lost, when even in the United States constitutional rights and society are in great danger threatened by totalitarian neo-liberal-globalist ideologies, it is the United States of America who we look at to carry the world out of totalitarianism again. The American constitution and the bill of rights stand as a beacon of freedom and hope for the whole world.

Imperfect as the United States are, with all its problems and contradictions, America is still the land of the free and of opportunity, and shall America's freedom finally fail, the whole world will hopelessly fall back into full-blown tyranny.

The internet has allowed information to freely flow, people may learn anything from anywhere, people may organize and help each other. With the internet a new form of money, better money has been created: bitcoin. People are able to save real sound money which cannot be controlled and diluted, people may economically interact with each other without having to rely on third parties and without government oversight, now sovereign nations may survive without the oppression of the IMF and World Bank and be truly independent. All this has become too dangerous for the ruling elites. The internet must be controlled, information must be surveilled, inconvenient speech must be censored and labeled as misinformation, hate speech, and conspiracy theories. People must be warned that bitcoin is a scam, rat poison, equivalent to gambling.

Governments and unelected international organizations partnering with the largest private corporations have decided that the public does not need freedom any longer and are best served by being offered safety.

9/11 has triggered the Patriot Act and mass surveillance, Covid-19 has triggered the end of bodily autonomy, the normalization of mass human gene-therapies, and introduced massive travel restrictions, digital surveillance, and dehumanization through face coverings. People should be up in arms because most of their freedoms are gone, instead they are scared of terrorism and viruses, and spend their time arguing about which political party is better and how to wear a mask properly.

People are no longer free, but they are safe! But the crude reality is that they are neither safe nor free, they are just slaves!

Money is the greatest army. I buy, hodl and use bitcoin first and foremost for my and my children's freedom.

> I came for the money, but I stayed for freedom, as money is time and time is freedom.

Chapter six: The never lost opportunity

I firmly believe that the overwhelming majority of bitcoiners came into the space to make money. There is no shame to it, it is just a matter of fact. Yet, I have tried to first and foremost make you understand what bitcoin is from a slightly technical and mostly philosophical prospective because long-term investors, the ones who have so far profited the most from bitcoin, are the ones who first seek to acquire understanding and then are able to increase their wealth significantly. Hopefully you will progress to the point that you will be a Bitcoin adopter and not someone who only tries to ride the waves for a quick buck yet, let me now talk about bitcoin as an investment.

Today it still puzzles me that there are so many people who say that they lost money on bitcoin, the only reason that this could ever happen is by not understanding bitcoin and trading it trying to get rich quick, buying during bull market frenzies and selling during bear markets as hopelessness seeps in, by making the easy mistake of investing your spending money expecting quick returns, or by falling victims of scams.

Just a word on scams: there have been many scams using bitcoin and crypto in general, I am sure there will be many more to come, but it is not bitcoin which is a scam, it's always centralized institutions which use bitcoin to scam people. Never confuse the tool with the perpetrator!

Understanding what bitcoin was built for is a prerequisite to increase your wealth. With bitcoin the greatest wealth transfer from the 1% to the rest of the population has begun and I hope you will choose to be a part of it. In fact, there are now many millionaires and even billionaires who understood and adopted bitcoin early enough, going from absolute poverty to great riches while there are bankers who keep on losing opportunities by refusing and actively fighting bitcoin, but this is for them a lost fight!

You might have lost the chance to get insanely wealthy by investing just a few dollars in bitcoin, but you still have the chance to build a solid prosperity for you and your family. Even nation states have today the historical opportunity to break loose of the neo-colonial slavery built on FIAT debt and corruption by adopting a bitcoin-based treasury system.

Until just a couple of years ago I often heard: "had I heard about bitcoin when it was a dollar, I would have bought it". Today I often hear: "had I heard about bitcoin when it was just ten thousand dollars, I would have bought it". The reality is quite different, and my reply usually is something like: "No, you wouldn't have bought it".

If you cannot buy bitcoin now when it is worth about a trillion dollars and is a well-established asset, you would have never bought it when its market cap was less than a million and the price volatility was off the chart". I have now enough experience to tell you that these are the same people who want to get in when bitcoin is off the chart and never invest in it when it is down by 50% or more. These are the same people who go after the latest "shit" coin they can buy for 30 cents thinking that it will be the next bitcoin and be worth $50K five years from now.

I also often get the question: did I miss the boat? During a recent business trip to São Paolo, Brazil, I had the opportunity to have dinner with a world-known cardiologist, and he asked me exactly this question: Roberto, did I miss the boat? Back then bitcoin was about $20.000 dollars. My answer was, as always: no! and I have given this answer at $10- 100- 1,000- 10,000 and even at $60,000. You might not have the financial possibility to buy a whole bitcoin today, but anyone can start saving little amounts and accumulate precious Satoshis. Bitcoin remains the best asset ever created with stable (yes stable!) returns no other asset can give you. My cardiologist friend is still on the sidelines, he could not have invested in bitcoin at

$20,000 and he could not invest in bitcoin at $60,000, now that we have seen the usual 70% correction, he thinks that bitcoin will go to zero. His fear is fueled by his lack of knowledge, and although I tried to teach him, no one can gain true understanding without being willing to invest the time, have an open mind and have some skin in the game.

Lessons:

Lesson number one: 1 bitcoin is 100.000.000 Satoshi, so anyone can buy a least a portion of a bitcoin.

Lesson number two: bitcoin, as valued in USD, is on a 13-year bull market! It's the gift which keeps on giving!

Lesson number three: Never think you have missed the boat. Once you understand what bitcoin is, you will know that it is never too late to convert part of your long-term savings into bitcoin.

Past performances are not guarantee for the future, but on a year-to-year basis the bitcoin performance in USD terms has no equals in history.

*bitcoin valuation in USD from 01-January till 31-December of each year as per my own research. Data may vary according to the information's source and method of accounting. This is no financial advise.

	Year	Beginning	End	% Change
1	2010	$0.05	$0.30	+500%
2	2011	$0.30	$4.72	+1,473%
3	2012	$4.72	$13.51	+186%
4	2013	$13.51	$731.95	+5,317%
5	2014	$731.95	$320.99	-56%
6	2015	$320.99	$430.21	+34%
7	2016	$430.21	$967.74	+124%
8	2017	$967.74	$13,896.63	+1,335%
9	2018	$13,896.63	$3,741.30	-73%
10	2019	$3,741.30	$7,197.53	+92%
11	2020	$7,197.53	$28,988.64	+302%
12	2021	$28,988.64	$46,399.79	+60%
13	2022	$46,399.79	16,538.91	-64%

In early 2023, as I write this chapter, one bitcoin is valued about $16,700. In the table above, I recorded the yearly closing values*.

As you can see by performing a simple statistical analysis of the chart above, bitcoin volatility is going down over time, although it is still by any commonly understood standards a very volatile asset. During the past thirteen years in USD terms, bitcoin has appreciated every year but three! So no, you have not missed the boat! Bitcoin is far from maturation and even if you start adopting bitcoin in 2023, you may still consider yourself an early adopter.

Lesson number four: do not get fixated on the USD value. Once you understand bitcoin, your goal is to save in Sats not in FIAT!

Lesson number five: bitcoin is a permissionless, decentralized digital monetary system with a fixed supply and fair rules for everyone. It is, by paraphrasing the great Andreas Antonopoulos (https://aantonop.com/): Rules Without Rulers. (I have no affiliation with Andreas whatsoever, I just like to mention him from time to time as he is truly a great teacher).

Decentralized means that it is not controlled by a single entity, but by a network of miners and nodes all over the world who guarantee the security and the reliability of the system. Bitcoin is the answer and the solution to an unsustainable FIAT debt system and government overreach which cause poverty, inequality, corruption, loss of freedom and the misuse of natural resources. A banker told me once that bitcoin is a Ponzi Scheme, bitcoin is actually the very opposite of a Ponzi Scheme as its supply is pre-planned and fixed, the FIAT debt system is the greatest Ponzi scheme ever created as an infinite amount of money is printed diluting your savings, and a fractional reserve system ensures that only a small portion of people's savings are actually available for withdrawal.

Bitcoin is pure monetary energy which can be transferred at the speed of light without having to ask permission to do so, it is money you can own and money you may spend because it belongs to you, because you have earned it with the sweat of your brows!

A final note: if left unchecked, the bitcoin USD valuation will go up almost indefinitely as long as FIAT money is infinitely printed. Expect strong pushbacks (directly and indirectly) from central banks and the establishment as they start feeling threatened. Push backs take the forms of wallets identifications, banning of mining and exchanges, taxation, price manipulation etc. These may lower the dollar price even for long periods, but I expect it to eventually bounce backs as countries are forced to unban bitcoin for strategic reasons. China, for example, has banned and unbanned bitcoin many times already. Also know that when there are strong financial down turns, bitcoin is not immune to them in the short run, but so far has always quickly recovered and I expect it to keep doing so in the future.

Understanding and forecasting bitcoin's price is extremely difficult if not impossible. There are many factors which play into it: supply and demand, adoption, trading, futures market, derivatives, active market manipulation, legacy financial markets, primary interest rate etc. This makes bitcoin volatile and unpredictable, although as we have seen from the 13-year data, its value tends to appreciate over time. However, be very skeptical of price predictions, of which the internet is full of. Personally speaking I tend to buy as many sats as I can during bear markets, when there is blood on the street and people are panicking. However, I always buy as much as I can afford to lose, and I always place my sats in cold storage. During frenzy times when even the cashier at your local supermarket talks about bitcoin, I try to unload some sats, but never all. I never try to pick tops and bottoms and I never sell all my bitcoin savings. At the end of the day, even if I skim off some of my stash, I always try to increase my bitcoin holdings long term.

This has been a good strategy for me, but again this is not financial advice.

There is a chance that bitcoin will go to zero or that it will underperform for a long period of time. History will tell, all I can do is to point out to past data as we talk about BTC evaluation in USD.

It is my firm belief however, that bitcoin is the alpha predator which will conquer the world by sheer superiority based on property rights, decentralization, security, and a limited supply backed by energy and CPU power.

Digitalization is a process which cannot be stopped, and it will fully engulf money. Bitcoin is the only digital gold, it is digitized, decentralized and independent economic energy.

The gene is out of the bottle,..... this such an exciting time to be alive!

Chapter seven: Bitcoin and the separation of money and state

Governments and empires have always used the ability to create money as their greatest source of power.

This ability allows the power structure to control and steer the economic output coming from actual work to achieve its independent goals. Unfortunately, the goal has never been the sole wellbeing of the population, but first and foremost the political interests of nation states, and often the private prosperity of governors, i.e. kings, politicians, and elite interest groups.

In practical terms, not only is taxpayers' money used for political purposes which go beyond the best interests of the taxpayers themselves, but money is always printed in quantities which always exceed economic growth creating inflation. Inflation, as we have already seen earlier in the book, is silent taxation and is an elegant stealthy way to transfer additional wealth from the working savers to their government.

Many times throughout history, the political structure (usually at the beginning of a new debt cycle) reassures its population that this time around money supply will be bound to a scarce commodity, usually gold. Slowly but surely, however, a crisis comes along which justifies the government's issuance of more money than it initially agreed to. Excessive money printing happens first so slowly and carefully that people only see the benefits of it, but as memory fades money printing accelerates until inflation becomes very tangible and a new debt cycle ends. As these cycles happen on a time span of many decades, people forget the lessons learned and history keeps on repeating itself with the silent consent of those who suffer the consequences the most, the people.

The only solution to this problem would be to separate the power of money creation from the state or government. This has been attempted many times, as mentioned, by tying the money supply to a scarce commodity, usually gold and/or silver. However, this system has never worked well because it is easy to cheat and circumvent. Governments may lie about how much gold reserves they have, gold coins may be shaved off or counterfeited, and political circumstances may conveniently justify the "temporary" use of the printing press for the common good.

With digitalization, decentralized protocols and blockchain technology which guarantees true transparency, technology has provided us with a tool to ensure that governments stick to the rules. However, it is clear that people who hold power will try anything not to relinquish the right of money creation (i.e., issuing debt) and it is therefore clear what motivates politicians, bankers, and elites to dismiss bitcoin as a Ponzi scheme, money for terrorists, drug dealers and pedophiles. Assertions which become ironic once you realize that FIAT is the biggest Ponzi and that FIAT provides terrorists, drug dealers, and armies with the very resources to exist.

Bitcoin has been invented and released to carry us through a freer world. Bitcoin is not only money which may be transferred peer-to-peer at the speed of light, it is not only censorship-resistant and virtually unconfiscatable, bitcoin is not only the most secure digital asset protected by an incredible amount of CPU power and energy, but bitcoin's monetary policy has been indelibly printed in its core consensus protocol and can never be changed, not because it is physically impossible to change, but because modifying it will mean the creation of a new kind of bitcoin all together. Bitcoin is therefore eternally immutable.

With bitcoin who governs us can no longer change the rules to accommodate political, strategical interests or the usual crisis. Politicians, kings, and governors will only be able to collect money through direct taxation, which has clear limits of acceptance.

Bitcoin represents the only way to achieve separation of money and state.

Politicians such as Nayib Bukele, once they accept bitcoin, relinquish the power to use monetary policy for their own benefit. This is for me the ultimate proof that President Bukele works for his people and only for his people.

Real wealth, freedom and equality can only be achieved by fixing the money. You might see inequality, poverty, famine, pollution, and wars. Surely, they are caused by corruption, lack of education, lack of basic healthcare, egoism, and true evil, but those are not the root-causes of the problems but just symptoms. The root issue is always fake money, created for the benefit of the few and the enslavement of the many! Only FIAT money printed as debt may be used to rage wars, corrupt people and organizations, secure political power and acquire real assets literally ransacking entire nations.

What the world needs is a decentralized money system which will guarantee fair rules for everyone and protect the working class through individual freedoms.

Let me please explain to you what I mean by "decentralized" and "fair rules".

Decentralized means that no one owns the asset and/or the network. No single nation, entity or group can either change the money supply or the governing rules. Participants within the network can interact peer-to-peer without the need of intermediaries as the system itself guarantees that interactions are trusted.

Fair rules means that the rules have been written and encoded in the so-called consensus protocol, no one can just unilaterally change them. Rules affect how transactions are registered, how the network is organized, how miners are paid and how money supply is regulated. As rules are enforced by the decentralized system, it is rules without rulers, a pre-established fair and incorruptible financial order.

Sound money which cannot be monopolized to serve the interests of the few, is the keystone to building a real free economy, the free economy which Adam Smith envisioned in its book, "The Wealth of Nations". Even the American constitution, which unfortunately has been deeply weakened and undermined, mentions the use of gold and silver, or sound money. Today the world is digital, and bitcoin is the only existing form of sound and incorruptible digital money.

Maybe you never thought about money in a non-monopolistic way. Why should the government be the only one to be able to generate money and to write the rules on how money is created and distributed? Do you think that a free economy, which is the only kind of economy which generates true wealth, may really be free if the medium of exchange is already monopolistically controlled?

The only way to really build a free economy is to start by freeing the money and allowing the unleashing of real sound money with unchangeable fair rules for everyone.

You can only Build Back Better when nation states will finally experience the separation of money and state.

As I said, the gene is out of the bottle and cannot be undone, no matter how governments react, people may now choose how and with what to interact with each other and this will force the establishment to accept that they no longer hold a complete monopolistic power on money. You might see the covid pandemic and the resulting technological technocracy leading us in the opposite direction, but maybe this is just a desperate attempt to stop the ultimate freedom, monetary freedom, from becoming a reality.

With bitcoin and the blockchain revolution, prosperity will reign through innovation, free and frictionless economic exchange.

I believe, although I can surely not speak for him, that this is the very reason Satoshi released bitcoin! Money and power are the root of all evil but can also be the root of all good. We must allow sound, incorruptible money to lay out a solid foundation for a greater and fairer word.

I believe that humanity was never really free in its history. While the world today is not in a good place, I see the glass definitely more than half full.

Technology may be used for absolute control, but it is a double-edged sword. It allows us to create a world where people may interact with each other at the speed of light without borders and without censorship, technology allows us real monetary freedom.

First air travel, then the internet, and now bitcoin have all given humanity the chance to becoming really free for the first time in history.

Now that we are able to visit any corner of the world within a few hours of air travel, now that the internet has allowed us to freely communicate across the globe, separation of money and state would be the greatest thing humanity could achieve to progress towards real freedom. This is today possible for the first time in history by adopting a decentralized monetary system based on an incorruptible code, bitcoin.

Governments will only rarely allow the true separation of money and state, but it will come the day when they will be forced to do so by the sheer superiority of bitcoin.

Chapter eight: El Salvador and the volcano bonds

There are many countries in the world characterized by all or many of the following: low GDP, high national debt, high inflation rate, low average pro-capita income, poor living conditions, low life expectancy, high mortality, high birthrate, low average educational level, high crime, high corruption, large emigration rates. These countries are often called third-world countries or emerging economies. Whatever word choice you prefer, there is another aspect that is common among most, if not all, of these "poor" countries, they are all in a debt black hole.

Of course, these places are pretty much without exception all plagued by political corruption, but there is a mechanism in place to make sure that these countries remain poor, subservient, and politically corrupt. In order to finance their debt, these nations must borrow money by issuing high-interest bonds but will never be able to generate the economic activity to ever repay their debt. Particularly because debt is usually issued in US dollars, must be repaid in US dollars but is generated by economic activity in a local, weaker currency.

As a consequence, these countries are all funneled into accepting the help of the World Bank or the International Monetary Fund and are forced into a neo-colonialism financial state of subservience.

As people emigrate out of these countries to find better economic conditions, large quantities of human resources are also lost to "developed" nations which in turn profit from cheap labor. To add insult to injury, these developing nations are often also forced to sell their natural resources, land, and infrastructure to foreign entities to be able to survive. Consequently, these countries are usually unable to educate their own population, build economic infrastructure and are stuck in a spiral with no way out, a real economic black hole. On the surface the cause of these dire conditions is that they are governed by corrupt politicians, which (again) is mostly true, but the root evil is the FIAT money system and world organizations such as the IMF and the World Bank, which were initially instituted for good causes, but unfortunately have become tools to make sure that poor countries remain under financial bondage.

El Salvador is a small country in central America located on the Pacific Ocean bordering Guatemala, Honduras, and Nicaragua. Before it made news within the bitcoin community in 2021, I really did not know much about this country, all I knew was that it is mostly poor, probably corrupt and that the Salvadorian gangs such MS13 are among the world's most dangerous. Ironically and sadly, these Salvadorian gangs originated in the United States and were re-imported to El Salvador.

In 2021 El Salvador announced that it would make bitcoin legal tender and then, a few months later, announced a 10-year, $1 billion-bond carrying a 6,5% coupon: the Volcano Bond. Half of the proceeds would be allocated to buying bitcoin and half used for building infrastructure including geo-thermal energy extraction equipment and bitcoin-mining facilities powered by the many active volcanos present in this small country (hence the name Volcano Bond). Furthermore, President Nayib Bukele announced the plans to build bitcoin City, where citizens can start building bitcoin-based businesses attracted by 0% income tax, 0% capital gain tax, 0% property tax, 0% payroll tax, 0% municipal taxes, 0% CO_2 emissions and only 10% VAT.

Before going into the details, I wanted to commend this visionary young president hoping I will get to know him one day. I listened to one of his interviews on the famous podcast "What Bitcoin Did" with Peter McCormack (no association) and I can only say that I felt truly inspired by him. In this interview President Bukele talked about why he adopted bitcoin as legal tender, his plans to mine bitcoin using geo-thermal energy and his plans to issue bitcoin-backed bonds.

There, in a small country in Central America, a politician is doing something that could not only dramatically change the future of his country for the better, but the future of the whole world by leading the way; I feel honesty and good intents in President Bukele's words, and knowing the power of bitcoin to fix the world, I know that he is doing something good for his people's future.

El Salvador has a large dollar-denominated debt of about 23 billion dollars and has many of the attributes I listed at the beginning of this chapter when I tried to define "poor, third-world" countries. This large, accumulated debt keeps El Salvador under the bondage of its international institutional creditors, and has pretty much no way out of this financial bondage which, let's not forget, on the ground means no hope to improve people's lives.

The United States Federal Reserve's monetary policies are not only felt on US soil but also directly by those countries who use the US Dollar as their own legal tender such as El Salvador, which adopted the US Dollar in 2001. In President Bukele own words: "….when a country prints more money, there is a good side and a downside, the upside is that the government has more money to spend, the downside is inflation …., the problem with using an international currency which is not yours is that you are only absorbing the cost…., but you are not getting any of the new printed money". Clearly, as the Dollar supply has gone parabolic starting with the great financial crisis of 2008, El Salvador started looking for alternatives to edge inflation. The easiest alternative would have been the re-introduction of a local paper currency, but Pres. Bukele knew that a digital currency would offer a better solution for El Salvador, not only because the world is going digital, but because a bitcoin standard would offer many advantages in terms of inclusion, freedom and monetary strength derived by bitcoin's core values of pure decentralization, limited coin issuance supply, world acceptance and recognition. Furthermore El Salvador gets to use the bitcoin Lightning Network, which is hands-down the largest, fastest, most resilient and cost effective digital monetary network in the world for both digital payments and cross borders remittances.

El Salvador first adapted bitcoin as legal tender and then announced it will be issuing a 1-Billion Volcano Bond half of which will be directed towards bitcoin infrastructure. This is a historical event, in my opinion second only to the genesis block!

Before the Volcano Bond, El Salvador was able to finance its debt by issuing dollar-denominated Bonds with a coupon of 13%. By issuing the Volcano bonds, it would be able to immediately lower its Bond coupon down to 6.5%, payable in US dollars, and acquire an asset with a historical yearly return much higher than the 6.5% coupon rate. The Volcano Bond, as it is backed by bitcoin, would be considered "lower" risk, and provides the great historical opportunity for El Salvador to become not only debt-free, but overtime transform itself from a debtor to a creditor nation. The Volcano Bond provides the opportunity to build profitable and environmentally friendly mining infrastructure powered by geo-thermal energy and, with the creation of Bitcoin City, a place where crypto ventures may thrive, create well paid jobs and booster the local economy.

This is nothing short than revolutionary! I often fantasized about hyper-bitcoinization (the adoption of bitcoin by nation states), but seeing it happen before my own eyes is truly extraordinary.

For the first time in history a small, indebted "poor" country, which under the FIAT system has no chance of freeing itself from the debt bondage, courageously tries to help its citizens by reinventing the bond market. This is the way, the only way, that David can beat Goliath in the 21st century. Max Keiser (no association) tried to help Greece out of the ECB bondage and EU dictatorship by proposing this same strategy in 2011, a time when Greek people were suffering immensely as a result of poor decisions made by generations of corrupt politicians and by cruel conditions imposed by the ECB, through his then central banker Mr. Mario Draghi, the EU, and the IMF. Had Greece accepted Max Keiser's proposition, not only would Greece be debt-free by now, but it would have allowed the country to opt out of the Euro, it would have allowed Greece to prosper in freedom and independence, it would allowed the Greek to be sovereign, instead Greece is still under the EU's grip and the Greeks keep on suffering.

El Salvador is doing today what Greece could have and should have done 11 years ago. If president Bukele remains uncorrupted in charge and will be able to leave his post with a worthy legacy, Salvadorians will benefit tremendously in the years and decades to come, and this small central American nation will lead the way for many other countries towards monetary freedom. This can literally be the first creep in the dam that will lead to widespread hyper-bitcoinization, to true and long-lasting freedom and prosperity for the world.

If El Salvador is successful, I see other nations quickly follow in its footprints. The first to naturally follow will be "poor", small economically oppressed countries, the last to join would be the great powers as they have the most to lose. I see, however, the possibility that one of these great powers will want to position itself in a strategically advantageous position by overtly adopting bitcoin as a reserve currency. This logic might be interesting to Russia at it strives to find strategic opposing strength against NATO, but this is just pure speculation on my part, only time will tell.

Now you understand why bitcoin is so poorly regarded and often attacked by the ECB, the Federal Reserve, and the IMF. Bitcoin is nothing short of a direct natural threat to their power. Bitcoin's core values of pure decentralization, censorship-resistance, un-confiscatable fixed supply backed by CPU power and energy make it incorruptibly strong, a strength which exists only to serve the people and not the elite.

Once you take away the ability of printing money out of thin air from central banks, you give true power to the every-day working people, this is true democracy, this is true freedom!

President Bukele knows all this very well and by adopting bitcoin he has made the World Bank and IMF "mad" but paraphrasing his own words: "adopting bitcoin is really nothing different than having adopted the US Dollar in 2001, the difference is that in 2001 we did that to help the banks while now we are adopting bitcoin for the people".

Today, 70% of the people living under the Dollar FIAT system do not have a bank account and are excluded from the banking system, bitcoin allows immediate banking inclusion, and this factor alone will without a doubt improve people's standard of living.

President Bukele has shown respect for both the world bank and the IMF and has no intention of starting a fight with them (he says), he is aware that El Salvador needs to be part of the international community, yet he asserts the right of El Salvador to be sovereign and adopt measures which will help best its population. The IMF has already reacted with anger, first building the narrative that such a move by El Salvador is dangerous for the Salvadorians and now actively threatening that if El Salvador does not abandon bitcoin as legal tender it will "unfortunately" be difficult for El Salvador to raise dollars in the international markets. This kind of rhetoric, being southern Italian, reminds me of nothing else than the mob. When mobsters want to collect "the rent" from local stores the first thing they do is tell the store owner how dangerous the area is and offer protection for their own good; when protection is not paid the mob goes in and puts the store on fire...... after all the mob warned you that it was a dangerous area! The IMF seems to be acting as a legalized mob in dark suits, you better take their protection or something bad might happen.

Too bad for the IMF and its allies that bitcoin is the gene out of the bottle; It is out there, and no one can ever stop it, it will conquer the world by pure Darwinism for the benefit of the people. The goal of bitcoin is to take out central banks by giving power back to the people and overtake an antiquated and unfair monetary system through an incorruptible digital code. To achieve all this no politics or wars are necessary, it will occur naturally because bitcoin the asset is the hardest monetary asset ever created and because bitcoin the network is today (through the lightening network protocol) infinitively superior to the legacy payment and remittance network, as I said: this change will occur by pure Darwinism and cannot be stopped because of the pure decentralization and the natural monetary superior strength of bitcoin.

Another very important factor to mention about bitcoin as legal-tender law is that President Bukele never imposed bitcoin on its citizens, in fact buyers and sellers may exchange goods using either US dollars or bitcoin in a way that, for example, the seller may receive dollars even in the case that the buyer uses bitcoin. This was able to be done through the help of Jack Mallers and his company, Strike ® (no association).

Freedom, in El Salvador's bitcoin law, has been protected by a clear legislation without fine prints or ear marks which placed monetary freedom as the core value in a way that all citizens, no matter their preference, are protected. President Bukele did not even force the use of a governmental crypto wallet but allowed citizens their own choice.

This is what real freedom looks like! You give your citizens true options and allow every citizen to be its own captain. True equality should never guarantee equal outcomes but will provide equal opportunities and this is what bitcoin does.

The next few years will be extremely interesting. A successful Volcano Bond will open the way to a >$100 Trillion Bond Market which is today stuck in the 0% interest swamp.

El Salvador could become the Singapore of Latin America. As China bans (again) bitcoin, as Europe and the US tax bitcoin and Russia foolishly tries to ban bitcoin mining, El Salvador adopts bitcoin and starts attracting capital and talent from all over the world. Expect a brutal fight, but it is survival of the fittest and bitcoin is with no doubt much fitter than the debt based and corrupt FIAT monetary system and their legacy network. This will be even more true once the legacy system will put on the "digital currency suit" of CBDCs, for which I dedicated a special chapter.

The legacy powers will fight back, but David will win! Goliath just does not have a chance!

Bitcoin has opened the world to monetary blockchain technology, and people will use it at an ever-increasing pace. Whether governments like it or not, people have a choice now and they will pick how to spend and how to save from a basket of different blockchain offerings, including government CBDCs.

El Salvador means "the Savior", maybe it is not that casual that hyper bitconization is starting there.

Chapter nine: bitcoin vs CBDCs, the battle between freedom and total control

The word "digital currency" is representative of both CBDCs (Central Bank Digital Currencies) and bitcoin, but the comparison stops there.

All digital currencies offer their users many advantages in storage, transaction speed, counterfeiting protection, usability etc., they may be kept in an electronic wallet within a phone or a watch, and be used in any store for contactless payments. The wallet may also be kept on a PC for online payments bypassing credit-card fees and third-party risks.

When the central bank becomes the issuer of a digital currency, there are also other properties which are extremely useful to the issuer: ease and speed of monetary policy implementation, programmability, data collection, tax collection, anti-money-laundering, anti-tax-evasion, and prevention of other illegal activities.

When it comes to monetary policy implementation and programmability, CBDCs allow central banks to implement interest rates changes at a lightning speed and creates the ability to collect highly accurate data and surgically adopt monetary policies.

Differentiated interest rates could be tailored for different age groups, sex, income bracket etc. If a central bank would want to incentivize spending of retirees, and at the same time incentivize saving for 25-35 years old, CBDCs would allow to set a different interest rate for those different groups of individuals. In another example, if the central bank would want to incentivize spending during the Christmas season, a monetary stimulus may be given by providing money to citizens that is tight to an expiration date, to a certain kind of products or even to a specific geographical location. These are just two theoretical examples of how CBDCs could be programmed to serve and tailor monetary policies goals.

CBDCs will provide an incredible amount of valuable real-time data on who, how and when is spending money for the benefit of real-time policies optimization. CBDCs, once universally used and in the absence of cash, may also be easily used to curb any illegal activities.

CBDCs will also allow the deleveraging of the financial system and will also not allow bank runs anymore, as cash will be "retired".

This is all great! Who would not want an easy-to-use money, particularly if free lunches are handed out, and who would not want to block illegal activities?

There are however important nuances to the careful eye which need to be pointed out and which should not be quickly dismissed. First and foremost, CBDCs are FIAT currencies created as debt but in a native digital format, they are controlled by a centralized entity which has full control and authority over it and give central banks literal superpowers. CBDCs will be issued directly by central banks to private citizens bypassing private commercial banks creating a direct monetary connection between the government and its citizens. As CBDCs are a digital form of FIAT money, the greatest Ponzi Scheme ever created, the working class and the third world will continue to be robbed for the benefit of governments and multinationals; however, governments now have the power of total control because CBDCs not only allow them to steer consumers spending, but may also be used to hinder payments and spending as punishment for noncompliance or political dissent. The devil is, as always, in the details!

A blatant example is the 2022 Canadian truckers' freedom-convoy protest again. As I write this chapter the Canadian government not only froze their 10 million CAD crowd funding, but just announced that it would freeze all bank accounts of all protest participants and their donors.

With CBDCs and AI in place, tyrannical total political and behavioral control will soon become exponentially easier. A license plate is scanned and matched with the owner of a protester, cameras with face recognition acquire data on dissenters, AI scans for opposing views and "disinformation" posted on social media or even privately spoken at the presence of a listening device..., and all CBDCs connected to those individuals are frozen instantly, of course.... under the pretest of terrorism and money laundering, peace, safety and the common good!

Let me give you another example, I had Covid-19 in November 2020. This allowed me to develop long lasting immunity to corona viruses as proved in many scientific publications. As the Austrian (I currently live in Austria) government mandated vaccinations on everyone, I was not allowed to do anything besides work from home and grocery shopping. Today, as I write this chapter, I am not allowed to buy a pair of jeans or to get a haircut. These measures are clearly not health-related but are draconian totalitarian measures meant to coerce me to take a medical treatment which I do not deem necessary. I still was able to get haircuts from a friend of mine paying cash, and I was able to get me a pair of used jeans paying again ...with cash. If CBDCs were already in full swing and with no cash available, as an option as I fully expect a ban on cash, I could never get a haircut nor a pair of jeans, I could probably not even get paid for my work or I would not be able to fill my car with gas. The government would have total control over anyone with critical or dissenting views. These are superpowers that Hitler, Stalin and Mussolini only dreamed of, they allow for immediate policy compliance and bankrupts anyone who dares to independently think.

CBDCs are not inherently a bad thing, but in the hands of nefarious actors, which history books are full of, and if left unchecked are the ultimate weapon of mass control. Do you think for a second that governments who today are coercing people in giving up their bodily autonomy by negating basic services would hesitate to use digital programmable money as a weapon? I hope you are not naive enough to think so, and I hope you are not so stupid to think that nefarious governments are only relegated to history books or just a problem of the Middle East, Asia or South America. CBDCs are a financial weapon which would have made life for our current political leaders, their devastating and totalitarian draconian policies much easier to implement. Of course, all in the name of health, justice, security, safety, equality, inclusion, democracy and the common good!

As already mentioned, bitcoin is also a digital currency (although bitcoin is really only a currency in El Salvador today) but the comparison stops here simply because bitcoin is the complete opposite of CBDCs. First of all, bitcoin is decentralized and as such cannot be controlled by single entities, it also has a limited supply against the silent theft of inflation and cannot be easily and infinitely used to gain political power. Furthermore, people may take ownership of it, the same way one takes ownership of physical cash, allowing peer-to-peer transactions.

Bitcoin is the epitaph of freedom and private property whereas CBDCs can easily become a tool of total control and surveillance.

Once CBDCs are issued, bitcoin will be the only way to use sound digital money and avoid total control. My belief is that as CBDCs are rolled out, bitcoin will be programmed in a way that it can be cross exchangeable with CBDCs for everyday purchases. Only if cash, CBDCs and bitcoin are allowed to coexist, we will have the nefarious powers of CBDCs in check!

While the internet has democratized information, blockchain has democratized money. Attempts to censor information flows on the internet by banning, shadow banning, and propaganda "fact-checkers" have not only miserably failed, but backfired. In the same way, block-chain technology has and will democratize money in an unstoppable way. Any attempt to ban mining and exchanges has failed and any further attempts to curb this technology will only incentivize further adoption.

Bitcoin and the innovations which it ignited (Lightning Network, stable coins, defi etc.), will only threaten central banks and governments' power if those institutions will actively try to forbid them. Governments will be much better off allowing the coexistence of both systems and should only regulate centralized institutions with the purpose of avoiding blatant scams. If governments will allow a legal and correct freedom of monetary choice, wealth creation will increase as a direct natural result of freedom and commerce.

I often hear people say that CBDCs must be stopped, that we should pay cash and store gold to counterweight CBDCs. These positions are not only anachronistic but ineffective. You cannot stop CBDCs, the same way that you cannot stop AI and self-driving cars. People only need to realize that just as democracy and freedom are best defended by the balance of power and by allowing opposition, so is monetary freedom best guaranteed by balancing the central banks' powers. There is only one way to balance the power of Central Bank Digital Currencies, and that is through a decentralized digital currency which allows for peer-to-peer transactions: bitcoin!

This is the reason why people need to adopt bitcoin, not to necessarily make more FIAT, but because it is our only ticket to freedom.

Chapter ten: bitcoin, ALTs and stable coins. Can a better bitcoin exist?

As bitcoin went from a few cents to thousands of dollars, many alternative crypto currencies (ALTs) have evolved over time. Some wanted to be a better bitcoin, some wanted to achieve things which bitcoin was not designed to achieve, and most were created as pure rug-pull scams or Ponzi schemes, illegal securities.

In the past, many critics have pointed out that bitcoin transfers are slow and expensive to be a unit of exchange, that bitcoin is too volatile to be a unit of account and that bitcoin consumes too much energy to be sustainable and environmentally acceptable.

The question which quickly often came during the first years of bitcoin and which many still ask today is, can a better bitcoin exist? Some say never, some say that bitcoin is already a crypto relic. Who is right?

The better question is what are you trying to create? If the answer is money, then the other question is, can you create a form of money which is better than bitcoin? But better in what? faster transaction speed? lower transactions fees? better decentralization? lower energy consumption? better privacy? DeFi programmability? NFTs programmability? Etc.

My straight short answer is no but let me please explain you why.

If your goal is to create electronic cash, digital gold which can move at the speed of light, is protected from inflation, is completely decentralized, is secure, censorship-resistance and unconfiscatable, there is no way around bitcoin's proof-of-work protocol. People have created crypto currencies which are faster than bitcoin, are more scalable than bitcoin, have lower transaction fees than bitcoin, have lower energy consumption than bitcoin, but none of these ALTs have all the core values of bitcoin and are therefore not, nor will ever be digital gold: hard, sound money in cyber space.

For bitcoin to remain the digital gold reserve, hard, sound money of the digital era, none of these core values may ever be sacrificed. As soon as you try to improve any aspect of bitcoin by sacrificing one of its core values you will no longer have the digital gold reserve monetary power status.

Early bitcoiners remember well the block-size war. Proponents of faster, cheaper transaction and scalability wanted to adopt large blocks size, opponents rejected the idea as large blocks size would have meant that only large data centers would have had the technical capabilities of running full nodes. As the existence of thousands of nodes is a key aspect of full decentralization, large blocks-size were rejected.

Today I, and many other bitcoiners, are happy that we were able to preserve decentralization because full scalability has been reached through technology using a second-layer solution, the Lighting Network®.

Energy consumption is an issue until you understand that energy is never created or destroyed but only transformed, we need energy to create and protect hard, sound money! If you do not understand this concept, you do not understand bitcoin. Yes, we need environmentally clean energy, yes.... miners' computer chips may be optimized for energy consumption, but digital gold is no longer digital gold without energy consumption and CPU power.

Another issue is privacy. Many people falsely think that bitcoin is anonymous, but this is not true. Any public address may be queried because bitcoin's blockchain is an open ledger. As soon as a public address is connected to an identity there are no secrets, it is like being able to see the account balances and movements of any bank account by just knowing someone's account number. Bitcoin was never built to be stealthy like Monero®; it could become stealthy, if necessary, but today it allows for full transparency. The reason for this is that bitcoin was built to be sound money, allow freedom of exchange, protect privacy, promote financial transparency, but was never meant to guarantee secret payments.

Bitcoin guarantees censorship- and confiscability- resistance and enough privacy for most people. Will bitcoin become stealthy? Yes, very quickly if governments will force bitcoin into that, but today is not necessary.

Technological innovations, such as the Lightning Network, must allow improvements to bitcoin without ever compromising bitcoin's core values.

It is now clear that proposals for a better bitcoin have failed and always will. However, some ALTs have good reason to exist when they provide useful innovations. DeFi applications, for example, allow crypto owners to lend and borrow, create an infinite number of applications such as insurance, digital ID networks, and decentralized banking.

Another innovation that has changed the crypto industry are stable coins. These are crypto currencies, decentralized and centralized, which are pegged to the USD by reserves or by cryptographic codes. Crypto owners may exchange some of their assets for stable coins and are able to gain interest on them by providing liquidity to exchanges or may spend them through credit cards at any store. Stable coins are the bridge between the crypto world and the real everyday economy based on FIAT money and allow users to completely bypass the need of the traditional banking system. Example of stable coins are Theter, USDC and DAI (just to mention a few).

Warning: stable coins are new, mostly supported by centralized entities, and are not fully audited. Furthermore, stable coins are currently under strict scrutiny by many governmental officials as they constitute a direct threat to monetary sovereignty much more than bitcoin.

In conclusion, no other proof-of-work or proof-of-stake alternative protocol will ever replace bitcoin as sound money or digital gold. Some, although very few, ALTs provide great added value to the crypto space in other areas and are overall good for the industry; however, I consider bitcoin as the only free cryptographic form of hard, sound money. ALTs are, in my opinion, are investment opportunities the same way private companies' stocks are, be aware however that most ALTs are de-facto illegal securities. Furthermore, if a stable coins and DeFi protocols will be built around bitcoin, I really see little reason for any alternative coins to exist.

Chapter eleven: bitcoin and energy consumption

Earlier in the book I explained why the bitcoin network with its proof-of-work protocol requires a lot of energy. I would like to dedicate an extra chapter at this regards as this is a crucial concept to understand. I do not hide the fact that when I first heard about bitcoin's energy consumption, I was completely shocked, I found such energy consumption completely unnecessary and bad for the environment. It has been estimated that in 2022 alone, the bitcoin network will require about 200 TWh of electricity; this is comparable to the actual energy consumption of entire countries such as Thailand or Poland. But why does bitcoin use such a large amount of energy and, more importantly, is it really necessary?

According to the law of conservation of energy, energy in neither created nor destroyed, energy is only transformed.

Everything in this world is based on energy. The energy I need for my organs to function come from the food I ingest and my ability to use oxygen, my food comes from the grocery store which used energy to sell it to me, the grocery store got it from the delivery truck which used energy to deliver it, the truck got it from the factory which used energy to process it and package it, the factory got it from the farmer which needed energy to raise cattle or grow vegetables, the vegetables used energy from the sun to absorb nutrients and grow. Everything on earth exists as a consequence of energy which is ultimately the energy coming from the Sun.

Gold also needs lots of energy to first become gold in the form of a rock, and then for extraction, refinery and finally to be stored, transported and protected.

There is nothing on earth which does not require energy; However, as mentioned energy is never just lost but transformed and the question is not about energy consumption but if that consumption is of utility.

bitcoin also needs energy, and we will learn that it is energy itself which provides bitcoin with intrinsic value and security.

Imagine a digital field where coins may be mined, now imagine that these coins may only be found at a pre-determined rate and are limited in number. Paul and Ann go to the field owner and say that they would like to work on the field extracting coins. The field owner tells Paul and Ann that they are welcome to mine coins, but by doing so they have to commit not only to mining but also to check that coins which are exchanged in the open market come from their field. Paul and Ann also need to commit to recording in a book all transactions they come across.

Paul and Ann accept and start mining using shovels, at first the mined coins have no value but after a few months people start thinking that the coins are worth something as they are limited in quantity and look nice. As the value reaches $1 dollar a coin, Paul and Ann start now selling the coins and people who bought them start using them to transact with each other. Every time that a transaction happens, Paul and Ann get a small percentage of it in fees, in exchange they check that the transacted coins are legitimate and document the transaction. As the value of the coins increases, more people ask the field owner permission to mine, the owner welcomes anyone who mines, checks, and documents transactions, the field is open to everyone he says, but underlines the fact that miners must all abide by the same rules, and that the coins are limited: only so many can be mined in an hour till a maximum number of coins have been extracted all together. The miners perceive that the field is very precious, people now come mining not only with simple shovels but with more and more sophisticated machineries; furthermore, miners build a fence so that thieves may not come in. Now for a thief to come in to steel coins has become very complicated, while at the beginning there was only Paul and Ann with two shovels, now there are thousands of people with very high-end machineries protected by cameras and trained dogs; stealing has become almost impossible. Cheating the system is also impossible, if one of the miners falsifies any documentation, the other miners will automatically see it and reject the documentation. By doing so, the occasional dishonest miner ends up doing the work without getting rewarded.

Bitcoin mining works exactly this same way. Miners provide computer power and use the energy to run their CPUs to mine a predefined number of bitcoin; furthermore, they check that the coins being exchanged into the market are legit, they confirm and document all transactions on the blockchain, which is nothing other than an electronic open ledger.

As the value and the number of users increase, so does the willingness of miners to provide computational power (a.k.a. hash rate) in return for freshly minted bitcoin and fees. There is a caveat though, as the hash rate increases so does the mathematical difficulty needed to adjudicate new blocks on chain. These two factors, more miners online and a higher difficulty cause an ever increase in energy requirements.

Simply put, miners are rewarded with coins in exchange for running and securing the network. Just like energy and equipment are required to mine, refine, and protect Gold, in the same way energy and computers are required to mine bitcoin and secure the network.

This mechanism makes sure that miners stay honest. If a miner will try to falsify a bitcoin transaction, the other 5 miners will see the dishonesty and will reject the fake transaction. In this case the dishonest miner has expended CPU power and energy without profiting from the transaction fee.

The amount of computational power and energy required by the network, secures it also from a so called 51% attack. In such an attack 51% of the hash rate would have to be used to create a double spending event which would de-facto nullify bitcoin's value by undermining its security. The attacker would have to dispose of

51% of the hash power and be able to provide the energy to run the hardware. The cost of such attack, if at all possible, runs into the billions of dollars. That means that someone would be willing to spend tens of billions of dollars to attack the system which would then be rendered worthless. The only actor who would have the motive and capabilities to do so are large nation states acting undeterred at the global level. However, as we will see later in the book, there are countermeasures which would make a 51% attack even by an evil-intended nation state, extremely unlikely.

This is the reason why the bitcoin network requires so much energy; energy and CPU power are needed to create digital gold and secure the network from attacks and dishonesty while keeping it completely decentralized without the necessity of relying on a third party. Energy is therefore a necessity. In fact, if bitcoin were to require no energy and no CPU power, it would be worth nothing!

But is it worth it to spend so much energy on a digital coin?

It depends! if you think that bitcoin is worthless, that is only a tool for speculations, then the energy used is worthless. If you think instead that the energy is necessary to secure a monetary system which will benefit humanity as a whole, then that energy has been put to very good use, it might as well be the best use of energy man can make.

Bitcoin is created and protected by energy, bitcoin is the power of the sun transformed into digital monetary energy which allows people to own digital money, to digitally save the sweat of their brows for the future and to transfer energy and value instantly across the world using a censorship-resistant, permissionless, and trustless network.

Now that I have explained this principle, let's get a little technical for the nerds out there:

The law of supply and demand will have that the cost of mining one bitcoin is equal to the cost of energy expenditures plus the cost of equipment which is equal to the USD value of one bitcoin.

Block Reward x Bitcoin Price = Hash Rate x Cost per Hash

This leads to an automatic self-adjusting system. Recently, in spring 2021, China banned all bitcoin miners, at the time about 70% of the global hash rate was located in China. As the miners went offline, the hash rate dramatically decreased, but so did the algorithmic difficulty. As a result, old miners were put back online and new mining opportunities were filled in places such as Texas. This is a blatant example of the resilience of the bitcoin network which can respond to any crisis automatically. Only a few months later the global hash rate came back to its previous levels through the simple effects of free-market's supply and demand. Here is the bitcoin USD valuation and the hash rate curtesy of glassnode.

As you can see from this graph (source: blockchain.com), the hash rate is constantly increasing, the big drop in 2021 was the China-ban which resolved itself within just a couple of months.

Hash Rate
196.4 EH/s

China Ban

2009-02-02   blockchain.com/charts   2022-02-21

Bitcoin offers a censorship-resistant, permissionless, and trustless network which allows store and transfer of value through peer-to-peer digital cash by means of an open and decentralized proof of work protocol.

An alternative to bitcoin needs to support all these features in a more energy-efficient-way. But there is no alternative as proof of work ensures that attacks on the network are too costly and allows for conflict resolution in case of a chain split because energy is a stake. In addition, the proof of work mechanism minimizes trust since the valid chain, the one with the most accumulated work, may be easily proven by anyone. These aspects make proof-of-stake, today, a non-viable alternative although it could become viable once mining is over or to temporarily protect the system during a 51% attack.

Work is energy directed to a certain action and energy is "work done," as stated by the French mathematician **Gaspard-Gustave de Coriolis**. The work done can be stored as hard-sound money, bitcoin, for future expenses or spent in exchange for goods and services.

At the end, bitcoin is stored energy which can be used through time and space to acquire goods and services, to generate economic value. This makes bitcoin unique as digital gold.

The fact that bitcoin uses vast amounts of energy is not a case against bitcoin, quite the contrary! bitcoin is secured digital Gold which can serve, just as Gold, as the reserve digital energy needed for a modern and fair monetary system. Energy use is therefore a necessity to secure something of immense value for the world and humanity.

Of course, energy may be obtained in sustainable ways, bitcoin de-facto incentives the transformation of energy in the cheapest and therefore always more often in the most environmental way possible. Furthermore, as excess electricity may not be conserved, bitcoin is the perfect way to use energy which would have otherwise been wasted.

There is also another aspect to take into consideration, which most people completely ignore. The current debt-based FIAT system encourages wasteful consumerism. Think about of all the cheap t-shirts people buy because they are just $5 apiece. These t-shirts were produced by using cheap fabric, lots of chemical products and probably child labor; After production, these t-shirts are then transported for thousands of miles in large containerships burning raw dirty diesel fuel. These t-shirts are then often worn once or twice and then thrown in a closet full of more cheap clothes until people decide to dispose of them; at the end most of these items will be burned releasing heat, smoke, and chemical pollution. Cheap FIAT money has driven the world to extreme consumerism, harmful production, and slave-labor, causing both toxic pollution for the environment and human enslavement. Now, if bitcoin would be adopted as our monetary system, people would no longer buy cheap t-shirts, in fact they will probably buy fewer t-shirts but only quality items, as they would only want to exchange precious money for good quality products. Seen in this prospective, bitcoin would also allow the world to use energy much more efficiently as a whole and prevent the release of unnecessary polluting agents through production and transportation.

Another important factor is that bitcoin mining tends to use the cheapest possible energy source, and this is becoming more and more excess energy that would otherwise be wasted. The big problem with energy is not energy production, but it is energy storage. Think about flaming at gas mining facilities, or excess gas extraction which cannot be transported and stored and can only be burned for no benefit. Think about renewable energy from windmills and solar panels, this is produced when wind is blowing and sun is shining, yet this is not necessarily the time when energy is needed. As storing all this energy is too expensive or impossible, a lot of this produced energy is discarded. Bitcoin mining is being used more and more to pick up excessive energy during low-peak consumption times and may also be reduced or turned off during times when energy is needed elsewhere for other purposes. In this contest, bitcoin mining may stabilize and strengthen the energy grid system. An example has been Texas during a winter storm in late 2022. Texas is home to many mining companies which use cheap excessive energy. As a winter storm crippled energy supply, miners went temporarily offline and effectively stabilized the grid. The world is turning electric, and bitcoin is the monetary system which not only provides real, secure, hard-sound money, but will also help strengthen and stabilize the ever-growing world power grid.

In conclusion, bitcoin's energy consumption is justification for a fair monetary system based on decentralization, fixed supply, and security. The energy used to create and protect bitcoin gives it intrinsic value and security. Bitcoin represents stored energy and stored work in the form of digital gold. Energy consumption should not be seen as a negative, everything in the universe requires energy to work and create value of any kind. As sustainable energy production increases, the cheapest energy forms become excess energy of renewable sources, at this regard bitcoin helps strengthen and stabilize energy grids without contributing to pollution.

Chapter twelve: Be your own bank

We have discussed that bitcoin is the true beacon of monetary freedom as it is hard, sound money which you may own, save, and spend. bitcoin allows monetary inclusion in a world which still keeps out 70% of its people from basic banking services.

When you buy into bitcoin you may decide how much ownership you are willing to take, from no-ownership and only price exposure, to full ownership in cold storage.

If, for example, you decide to buy Micro Strategy's stocks, you own a piece of a company which is heavily invested in bitcoin, and you are indirectly exposed to bitcoin´s price action without having to own the asset itself. This might be an option for a long-term investor who regularly invests in stocks but is not interested, or is not capable, of taking direct ownership and responsibility of bitcoin.

Another option is to buy bitcoin from a provider such PayPal®. In this case you buy Sats, but you cannot move them out of the PayPal® system (at least at the time of writing). In this case, you are directly exposed to bitcoin´s price action, but you are really buying a derivative, you are not allowed to take full ownership of the coin. This method is recommended for people who want to gain direct exposure to the asset's price but are not willing to take either ownership or responsibility yet are enough computer savvy to use an electronic payment system such PayPal.

Another option would be to purchase your coins from an accredited exchange such as Coinbase® or Kraken®, just to name a couple (no association). When using this option, you are really acquiring ownership of the asset and you may choose to keep the asset within the exchange, or you may decide to export ownership of the coins to a self-controlled wallet for which you own the private keys. In both cases you own the asset, but you have different risks and benefits which we will now discuss.

If you decide to leave your Crypto within the exchange, you own the asset, you are exposed to the price' action, and you have full access to the exchange's customer service in case of need; however, you run the risk that your funds become frozen (by decision of the exchange or the government), hacked or lost if the exchange goes out of business. Old bitcoiners will remember how Mount Gog, located in Japan, at the time the only exchange in the world, was hacked with the result that all bitcoin within that exchange were stolen.

Instead of leaving your bitcoin within the exchange, you may decide to take full ownership of your coins by exporting your coins to your private wallet. In this case, you not only have full ownership of your coins but also take full responsibility of the coins by self-storing them.

Taking direct ownership has at least two variants. You may keep your asset on a hot wallet, which is a wallet connected to the internet, or you may keep your coins in cold storage, which is a wallet not connected to the internet, or at least not always connected to the internet.

A hot wallet may be kept on your phone (or your computer) and is a very convenient method to store and spend your coins. The disadvantage is, of course, that every time you are connected to the internet you might be hacked.

A cold storage wallet has a much higher level of security as your funds are mostly off-line and are only "hackable" once you connect the wallet to your computer. However, even in the case that you connect your cold storage device to the internet, to check your balance or to move funds for example, the computer chip governing the cold storage device is built in a way that does not allow external access to your private keys.

Another form of cold storage, deep cold storage, is keeping your private keys on paper or engraved on metal. The deep cold storage wallet is of course 100% safe from hacking but is very unfriendly to use, after all bitcoin is internet native!

Some people go as far as keeping private keys split and buried in different parts of the world to keep funds secure.

Another option to increase the safety of your funds is to use a multi-sig wallet which requires multiple signatures whenever funds are moved.

What is the right way to store bitcoin? That really depends on the kind of investor and user you are. Personally, I keep small amounts in hot wallets or directly on exchanges where I earn some interest, and I keep my life savings in cold storage. What is very important to me is full ownership of the coins. I am into bitcoin because I want to have my own money without having to ask permission to use it, without having to fear governments, banks, or companies to freeze my funds. With ownership, however, comes great responsibility!! If I have a problem, there is no customer service which may ever help me recover my funds.

I am my own bank in cyber space with all benefits and responsibilities. I am sovereign! I can now save, lend, and borrow without having to ask permission. This is powerful, this can lift billions of people out of poverty, this is real freedom.

I am baffled by the amount of people who complain about the lack of freedom but are too lazy to take ownership of the coins. Bitcoin is about being sovereign, if you do not understand this you haven't fully understood the power of bitcoin. Surely technology needs to become easier to use, but it has already become much easier than just a 3-4 years ago. Don't be a trader, be sovereign, take ownership of your coins and use bitcoin not just as an investment but as economic energy to be saved and spent.

Chapter thirteen: The Lightning Network®

The Lightning Network® is one of the greatest innovations when it comes to bitcoin. To understand what the Lightning Network® is we need to understand what a layer 1 and layer 2 payment systems are which takes us back to gold.

Gold has been considered money for thousands of years because it is a reserve scarce metal providing underlying security and economic value. However, gold has some important drawbacks when it comes to functionality as a medium of exchange because it is hard to carry around, it is not easily divisible, expensive to store, and may be even counterfeited. During the gold standard, gold was kept into bank's vaults as an underlying security and banknotes were issued to simplify economic exchanges but were redeemable at any time for gold. This way people could easily carry banknotes in their pocket to buy goods and services and both the giver and the receiver of the banknote were sure that the note had real underlying value as it was redeemable for gold at any time.

You have to think of gold as layer-one money as it provides security of value, and of the banknote as layer-two money as it represents usability as a medium of exchange, yet they are fully exchangeable with each other.

Bitcoin as a layer-one money, just as for gold, provides security of true economic value. Bitcoin is optimized for decentralization and security at the cost of transactional speed, volume, and cost as an inevitable compromise. To improve usability as a medium of exchange, a layer two has been created for bitcoin in the same way that banknotes redeemable for gold were created. During the gold standards, banknotes were free to circulate but were not always redeemed for gold after each transaction. Making a comparison with the bitcoin network, it is like making transactions but not writing every transaction on the blockchain but only operate final settlements on it. This is how the Lightning Networkr® works providing fast, high volume and extremely low transaction fees.

The combination of the bitcoin and the Lightning Network allows now for both a highly decentralized and secured monetary system backed by bitcoin as the underlining asset (digital gold) and the functionality of a perfect medium of exchange for a now complete digital currency system. You can transfer any amount of economic value, from a fraction of a penny to billions of dollars, at the speed of light across the globe in a permissionless, non-censurable and non-confiscatable way.

The Lightning Network literally unleashes the true power of bitcoin as it provides instant payments, scalability, low cost and cross blockchains activity by adopting smart contracts and atomic swaps, this way transactions may be made off-chain with the confidence of on-blockchain enforceability.

The Lightning Network is an example of how technology can help overcome shortcomings of the bitcoin network without having to compromise bitcoin's core values.

The Lightning Network® is nothing short than revolutionary, it is nothing short than a disrupting technology which may be compared to the invention of emails at a time when communication was still done through letters and postcards. The Lightning Network® allows instant payments and remittances, almost for free, across the globe as peer-to-peer transactions. This will disrupt financial services such as Visa, Mastercard, MoneyGram, Western Union etc.

For more information about the Lightning Network, visit: https://lightning.network/#intro (I have no affiliation with either bitcoin or the Lightning Network).

Chapter fourteen: Reasons NOT to buy bitcoin

I have spent a lot of time and energy as an ambassador of bitcoin. bitcoin is a mean for individuals and nation-states to become debt free, financially independent, self-reliant, and outright sovereign. As much as I am a strong proponent of bitcoin, wishing that everyone would not only invest in it but fully adopt it, I also realize that bitcoin should be approached with a healthy dose of skepticism. True understanding of anything comes with both careful research and critical thinking as both are absolutely necessary for an objective evaluation of the bitcoin proposal.

During the years I have received many objections to bitcoin and even some accusations of fomenting sex trafficking, money laundering and unspeakable other crimes against humanity. Yet, it is exactly through the honest evaluation of such objections and accusations that I became convinced not only of the goodness of bitcoin but also of the absolute necessity of it to achieve real freedom. I am also convinced that those who make such accusations, either did not take the time to understand bitcoin, have an agenda or both.

Investors who do not go through the skepticism and critical analysis phase never stay bitcoiners, sooner or later they will leave the fold mainly because for these individuals, bitcoin was only a way to make more FIAT. These people are wiped out of the bitcoin's community map after the first 50% crash or the first scam they fall victim to, but these people were most likely never bitcoiners to start with.

True conviction can only come by asking skeptical questions about things that could go wrong with bitcoin. Understanding bitcoin's real potential and risks, whether real or perceived, is a must.

So let's go through some of these common objections:

- Governments may easily take out bitcoin by outlawing exchanges

To answer this objection, we have to go back in history when the only one exchange which existed was Mt. Gox in Tokyo, Japan. At the time it is believed that up to 70% of existing bitcoins were either held by Mt. Gox or transited through this exchange as an on-/off- ramp to FIAT. In February 2014 Mt. Gox suspended trading, closed its website and exchange services, and filed for bankruptcy protection against its creditors. The company later announced that about 850,000 bitcoin were missing and likely stolen.

As the only exchange in the world went out of business and with such a huge amount of bitcoin stolen, I realize that bitcoin should have never survived this event, but today bitcoin is still alive and stronger than ever! In 2017 China banned all crypto exchanges as well, this caused exchanges to migrate offshore, but it did not stop Chinese citizens from acquiring and trading bitcoin, in fact this caused only the Chinese government to lose its capability to acquire data from the exchanges. But what would happen if an international consensus of all major nations would unilaterally outlaw crypto exchanges? For such an event to materialize, all major countries such as China, the US, the EU and Russia would have to agree to simultaneously close all exchanges; at the same time none of these powers would overtly adopt bitcoin trying to achieve a strategic advantage. Let's imagine however that this would really happen, in this case the bitcoin USD valuation would be strongly negatively impacted in the short term, but somewhere in the world there will be a country which would allow new exchanges to pop-up in order to take advantage of the vacuum which was created. Also, DEXs (decentralized peer-to-peer exchanges) would start flourishing and replace centralized KYC exchanges. The result of this attack would be that small secondary countries would take advantage of the situation and people would be able to buy bitcoin through DEXs bypassing governmental controls. Large powers would lose data from exchanges, miss on taxes, and would allow small countries to raise up in power. I assume that sooner or later one of these major nations would break away from the agreement in order to build a competitive edge leaving their old allies with a huge lost opportunity. Such an attack against exchanges, even if coordinated, will never work and will only back-fire against their proponents. Countries know well that if such an attack were ever to succeed it must be done in a way to never leave any door open, but this is highly unlikely if not straight-out impossible.

- Governments may easily take out bitcoin by outlawing mining

China, after having banned exchanges in 2017, also banned bitcoin mining in the spring of 2021. With this event the hash-rate fell sharply almost overnight. Concomitantly, also pushed by Elon Musk's unfortunate tweets, the bitcoin price began a spiral from ca. $ 65.000 to $ 30.000. Until then, China had over 60% of the world's mining power. As soon as the ban came into effect, Chinese mining companies started immediately to relocate their CPU power abroad. The bitcoin network system is built to be incredible resilient; as the hash-rate collapsed the mining difficulty also significantly decreased, which resulted in people all over the globe taking out old mining equipment out of their basement and re-started to mine bitcoin with machines which had become obsolete and ineffective. At the same time, new mining companies started popping up particularly in the United States and Chinese mining equipment started to appear back online in countries such as Kazakhstan. Three months after the ban, the hash-rate was back at its peak levels and bitcoin reached again an all-time-high USD valuation of $69.000 in late 2021. The Chinese were again unsuccessful, they tried to push bitcoin away as they are implementing their digital Yuan, which is the people's money only by name when in reality it is a mean of total state control. Bitcoin survived just fine such a major blow and I am sure that Chinese citizens keep on buying bitcoin today through alternative routes. It was China as a country who lost the most, it first lost all bitcoiners' data by banning exchanges in 2017, and now lost their leading position in bitcoin mining which was worth many billions of dollars a year. I doubt that bitcoin mining will make its way back to China anytime soon. This is the perfect example to show that you may get your country out of bitcoin but never bitcoin out of your country.

Even if mining is outright banned from all major countries, which is at the moment unthinkable, bitcoin would only suffer temporarily and will definitely not only survive but continue to thrive. The China ban of 2017 and 2021 teaches us that if you want to kill bitcoin, you better not leave any door open as it will find it and continue to prosper again. Bitcoin's USD valuation might be volatile, but its hash rate keeps on going up regardless of its price.

- A 51% attack

A 51% attack consists of a majority of miners getting together and agreeing to act against the system by not approving transactions and re-writing past transactions. This would make bitcoin worthless as the security and trustworthiness of the system would be forever compromised. Private miners would never do that because it goes against their financial interests, a 51% attack would cost tens of billions of USD in equipment and energy, the attacking miners would be left, as a result, with a worthless bitcoin. Nation states would have the money and reasons to do such attack as they would want to eliminate a threat to their central banks. Provided that the attackers would be able to get the majority of the mining equipment under control and provided that the bitcoin network would not neutralize the attack on its tracks, a 51% attack would most likely be promptly identified and the remaining miners could group to decide not to accept any transactions coming from the corrupt pool, at the same time they could temporarily switch from proof-of-work to proof-of-stake until the attack is neutralized. The 51% attack was never (successfully) attempted against bitcoin when miners were few and the attack had a greater chance of being successful, today such an attack is very unlikely to happen and if it were to happen even more unlikely to succeed.

Again, if you are going to shoot the king make sure you will kill him, otherwise it will come back out stronger against you. A failed 51% attack against bitcoin will only prove to the world that bitcoin is un-attackable and immortal, it will be the best advertising for bitcoin you could ever make.

- Quantum Computer

A Quantum computer could take money from an elliptic curve digital signature signed transaction by reversing a transaction from a private key. The elliptic curve cryptography used in bitcoin is susceptible to quantum analysis, in fact according to my research a quantum computer capable of 256 qubits should be able to read a private key from a public address, which can be easily found in the block chain by reading transactions off a node. Besides the fact that such a powerful quantum computer is years away, the public key used to read the private keys must be from a public address where funds still exist. If you use a different public address every time you do a transaction, even such a quantum computer could not steal your funds. There are however many public addresses which still contain funds, the best example is Satoshi's stack. If Satoshi's coins were to move, we would know that a Quantum Computer with enough qubits has been created or that someone, of course, has Satoshi's private keys. The bitcoin algorithm is being however updated. The Taproot upgrade includes already a new signature algorithm, so as long as the system is updated to be quantum computer resistant, such a threat will never realize.

- Satoshi's coins

Many argue that if Satoshi's coins (about 1,1 million BTC) were to move, which they never did since he went offline, would crash the bitcoin market because of the supply shock and because we would know that Satoshi released bitcoin for personal gains. With every day that goes by, the possibility that Satoshi's stack moves is a little less, but if the coins were to really move the first question people would ask would be if a quantum computer had been created and placed in action. This is extremely unlikely because bitcoin algorithm will be quantum-computer resistance before the 250 necessary qubits are ever reached, and also because if someone had such a powerful weapon, which could be used to hack national strategic assets, it would most likely not declare it to the world by killing bitcoin first. We have to assume that Satoshi's coins would either never move because Satoshi is dead, or because he never mined those coins for personal gains (they are now worth around 50 billion USD). If Satoshi's coins were to move, the market valuation would suffer immensely from the supply crash, but it will eventually recover once those coins will be absorbed by the market. Another option, and this is my own "fantasy" speculation, is that those coins have been placed aside as a world reserve to be used as soon as the current corrupt system collapses and we are ready to rebuild a free world again on top of decentralized sound money: hyper bitcoinization's renaissance.

- Bitcoin damages the environment because of the immense energy expenditure

We have already discussed about bitcoin and energy requirements at lengths. Briefly, a proof-of-work algorithm cements the past as all past transactions cannot be re-written, this allows a digital monetary system to be strong, secure, and distributed by requiring energy. There is just not another way around it! bitcoin can therefore be seen as stored work in the form of a digital store of energy. If you think that bitcoin is useless, then all the energy expenditure is a waste, if instead you think that bitcoin is the digital monetary system of the future based on privacy, fungibility, censorship resistance, open access, neutrality, limited monetary supply, no intermediaries, and no rulers, then it is the most useful ever use of energy.

To look at this in another prospective, think about social media. The power consumption around its use is for sure tremendous, I imagine that it is more than bitcoin if you think about the whole pipeline from the infrastructures to the employees to the users' interfaces. Yet, is it useless energy? I would say no, it allows us to interact with each other, learn, get informed, buy and sell. This is just as true for bitcoin, is it just a coin which is exchanged for FIAT speculation? Or is a monetary system that empowers the world? In the latter case energy is no longer an argument.

Bitcoin's energy use must also be compared to the dollar system, whose energy consumption is not just the energy used to print banknotes, run computers, banks and ATMs, but includes all energy spent by the military-financial conglomerate to keep the dollar FIAT system afloat. The US dollar is backed by war, and this alone makes it the worse polluter of the world besides the fact that war, in a way or another, is always reprehensibly idiotic.

- Bitcoin is money for criminals and sex traffickers

I hear this accusation over and over again; it is a strange accusation which easily gets under my skin as I feel personally accused to be a criminal and a sex trafficker just because I use bitcoin.

Let's make this clear, a criminal who decides to use bitcoin is a pretty dumb one because all transactions are documented in an indelible, open, and auditable ledger, the blockchain. As long as we can associate a public address with a person (not that hard to do!) then there is no anonymity. In fact, bitcoin is NOT an anonymous system, it was never meant to be one; Bitcoin is a pseudonymous system. I am sure that some criminals used it and still do, but most likely they do not know how the system works. It is true that bitcoin was used on Silk Road in the past to sell drugs and other illegal activities, but as criminals came to understand that bitcoin's transactions are documented and that anyone running a node can see it, it became clear that other financial methods are better than bitcoin when it comes to criminal activities.

Besides, the greatest financial felons, money launderers and sex traffickers are multinational banks, pharmaceutical companies, politicians, and royals. That is well documented in many court rulings, and they all use the FIAT banking system.

This accusation is just a scripted narrative part of an information war trying to discredit bitcoin, full stop! Imagine if I told you that you should not use a car as it is used by criminals to make bank robberies. I think you got the point...

- Bitcoin will go to zero

I have heard this since bitcoin was $1,000! My only answer is that although past performances are no guarantee for the future, this claim has so far been false although it is in the realm of possibilities. Bitcoin will go to zero only if its security is breached or if the community would destroy bitcoin from the inside out by abandoning bitcoin's core values: privacy, censorship resistance, open access, neutrality, limited monetary supply, no intermediaries, no rulers, and full decentralization.

Other external governmental attacks will always trigger an evolutionary response. Not only the hash rate increases every time new players, even with a nefarious agenda, join the network, but if in need bitcoin may quickly become invisible, reactive, evasive, and vicious as any negative pressure which is unable to kill it, will strengthen bitcoin to the point of being virtually unstoppable.

Bitcoin is built to be attacked and becomes stronger with each attack.

Believe it or not there are as of today 441 (and running) obituaries of bitcoin according to the website www.99bitcoins.com

This is a fun website to visit, the mainstream media keeps on reporting the death of bitcoin since it was worth $0.23. This is clearly part of a scripted narrative supporting the FIAT-control agenda.

Bitcoin is a threat to the centralized FIAT financial system. The paid propaganda media, which has become nothing less than a prostitute for private and government interests, has discredited and attacked bitcoin so many times because bitcoin is simply a threat to the interests of their masters.

- Major governments will re-establish sound money

There is a non-zero chance that countries and central banks will restore sound money based on gold as a way to rebalance the economies and retore citizens' trust. If this were to happen bitcoin would no longer be needed or would only be there to make sure that central banks would not go back FIAT money again. The return of sound money could materialize, but I see it highly unlikely to happen out of benevolence and common sense, just because of the fact that such an event would inevitably force governments and militaries to become exponentially smaller; I see a possibility of this happening if enough countries chose bitcoin as a reserve treasury and legal tender, starting a wave that will wipe out large central banks and will force governments to either adopt bitcoin or to restore sound money in the form of CBDCs backed by gold. But even in the latter case, bitcoin would not go away completely to prevent governments to start cheating again.

Chapter fifteen: Who is Satoshi Nakamoto?

Satoshi claimed to be a 37-year-old male who lived in Japan, he was never seen or heard, his communication is limited to the genesis block Coinbase transaction on 03-JAN-2009 "Chancellor on brink of second bailout for banks" and technical posts on the bitcointalk public forum. People have speculated on the Satoshi's identity for years, some have pretended to be him, but no one really knows who he is or if under the name Satoshi a group of people are actually concealed.

Honestly, I do not care who he, she is, or they are…, all I know is that Satoshi was an incredible smart individual who wrote a decentralized monetary code which is not only a mastery of finance but also a masterpiece of cryptography still standing undeterred and secure today after 13 years.

Satoshi left us with the gift of real sound digital money. People today have the hope to be able to save again, to be able to retain and use the value of their work as they freely chose, without being afraid of the silent theft of inflation, of political censorship and persecution. Who would have suspected back in 2009 that bitcoin would have remained today the only way to save money and the only way to escape the governments' big brother omnipresence?

It is not only good but essential that Satoshi's identity remains concealed, it makes it impossible to attack bitcoin by attacking its creator. Satoshi left us with an incredible gift, which might ultimately be the gift of freedom. His last message was dated 07-MAR-14, it read: I am not Dorian Nakamoto. This message came as a surprise as Satoshi's posts stopped coming more than three years earlier and was considered just an act of mercy for Dorian Satoshi Nakamoto who was under investigation for being the bitcoin's creator.

I do not care who Satoshi is, I am just grateful for his gift!

I hope that by reading this book you realize just that. I walked you through the financial gains bitcoin achieved during the last decade, but that does not matter at all.

In today's world, bitcoin is the escape from a corrupt system, it is the escape of the digital prison being built around us, it is the escape from poverty and government dependance, it is the escape from tyranny and is the door to a better world.

This is what bitcoin is and I am grateful for Satoshi.

Chapter sixteen: bitcoin USD valuation analysis

Congrats! You made it through fifteen chapters without having read much about bitcoin's price and on how to make (FIAT) money with bitcoin.

This was done intentionally as the bitcoin's valuation is a result of adoption, and although important, it should not be the primary objective for its acquisition. If that is your sole purpose, you will never survive long as a bitcoiner.

In fact, this book has been so far mostly about the philosophy and history of bitcoin as a decentralized monetary system built for the benefit of the people, especially the working class, and it is a bastion of freedom and hope for humanity. Understanding what bitcoin is and what it stands for is of a magnitude more important than analyzing bitcoin's pricing chart trying to guess when to buy and when to sell to make more fake FIAT money. Of course, bitcoin can greatly increase your wealth, and it has done mostly so in the past decade, but that is not and should not be the purpose of adopting bitcoin. Let's not be however hypocritical, everyone wants to improve their living standards and there is a place and a time to do so by selling bitcoin for FIAT, but that is the result of believing in it and adopting it and should not be the main purpose, this is however an evolutionary process. The best you can do with some of your bitcoin FIAT gains is to acquire income-generating assets with it, this way you have put your sound-money savings to good work.

If your goal is to slowly increase your wealth using sound long-term strategies based on data, if your goal is to get off the hamster wheel which central banks placed you in when you were born, if your goal is gaining the ultimate freedom by adopting decentralized hard money, then please keep on reading as we now go deep into key charts analysis.

During my early bitcoin days, it was the up-side price performance which gave me excitement and made me feel like a superhuman investor. As I bragged about my crazy gains with friends and family, I pretty much ruined all thanks-giving dinners and Christmas parties I was invited to. Today it is not the upside which gives me the adrenaline shot, but quite the opposite! I know that bitcoin goes up overtime, so I only get really excited when bitcoin dumps because it gives me the opportunity to accumulate more sats. Today, while dumps give me excitement, capitulations are almost a sexual arousal experience! Everyone is a genius during a bull market, but it is during bear markets that a robust financial standing, strong ideals and discernment will make the difference.

Today, if someone asks me about bitcoin, I usually give an answer which sounds like this: Bitcoin is the greatest invention in history, if you want to invest in it, I will help you; However, please understand that you may lose everything and you should invest only what you are ready to lose; Understanding bitcoin will require about 100-300 hours of learning as an initial investment but if you stick to it, you might achieve financial freedom. Most people get turned off by my answer and never bother again whereas a few want to get educated and end up becoming real bitcoiners. Many will unknowingly become mass adopters in twenty years from now. People who come to bitcoin through hard work and who sticked in times of long and painful bear markets, are usually able to progress towards true financial freedom and independence, which takes time, determination, and commitment to build.

Bitcoin price: let's get it!

We have seen that if you objectively assess bitcoin's USD valuation through its 12 years history, you will very quickly find out that it goes only one direction, up! But why?

The reasons for this are two and work synergistically towards an exponential growth:

1) Bitcoin becomes more valuable as its utility, the number of users and the network's hash rate increase, and as innovations are made available.

2) Bitcoin becomes more valuable as the US dollar is debased by the printing press.

While these two factors result in price appreciation, there are factors who do the opposite:

1)   Short term speculation
2)   Finance structures as ETF and future markets
3)   Political and banking opposition
4)   Traditional markets status

When we analyze bitcoin's savage 12-year bull run we see that it is not linear but is rather characterized by fast peaks, disastrous drops, and long valleys: strong volatility.

Why is bitcoin so volatile?

The answer is complex. First, it is a fast-growing disruptive technology just like Amazon, Facebook, and Tesla whose stocks were also characterized by strong volatility as they initially exponentially grew.

On the other side of the equation, you also have governments who see bitcoin as a direct threat to their sovereignty and continue to ban it and unban it through legislation, then you have finance tools such as ETFs and future markets which use institutionalized trading to manage risk and manipulate the market, and finally you have powerful speculators.

To survive strong volatility, investors require deep understanding, strong stomachs, and diamond hands. Imagine an investor that considered the black Monday crash of 1987's S&P 500 drop of more than 20%, a life-changing event; How would such an investor react considering that bitcoin regularly sees drops of more than 30-40% during a bull market and has seen total drops of up to 90% many times during its bear markets?

Only an educated investor who understands the risks and benefits of such volatility can survive this environment and benefit from it. This kind of instable price growth must be seen as a necessary evil for a young, fast-growing and disruptive asset.

bitcoin's price evolution has 3 general phases: Bull Phase, Correction Phase and Re-Accumulation Phase.

A Bull Phase is a time to rapid price appreciation, a Correction Phase is a sharp decrease in price usually following an exponential growth phase. Last but not least, a Re-Accumulation Phase is a period when bitcoin's price lateralizes.

Technical Price Analysis gives you information about price, time, moving averages and geometrical formations but I personally use only very few long-term indicators to track bitcoin's price activity.

On-chain analysis is a crypto native tool. In fact, in crypto it is possible to see how coins are moving within the blockchain and exchanges, this data may be extrapolated to assess the market and even try making predictions.

There are tons of books written about technical analysis and there are on-chain resources who can help you gain inside on-chain intelligence, but both technical and on-chain analysis are not the purpose of this book.

As far as charts analysis go, I personally follow the KISS principle: Keep It Simple Stupid! I use the following charts to make me a picture of where we generally are.

Technical Price Analysis and models:

1) 20-Week Exponential Moving Average (20W EMA)
2) 21-Week Simple Moving Average (21W SMA)
3) 200-Week Moving Average (200W MA)

On-Chain Analysis:

1) Hash Rate

The 20-Week EMA (exponential moving average)and 21-Week SMA (simple moving average) represent the bull-market band. When the price is consistently above it, we are in a bull-market and the band act as a support, when the price is consistently below it we are generally in a bear-market and the band acts as a resistance.

The 200W MA (moving average) or even the 300W MA represents price bottoms, the closer we are to the 200W MA the less risky is an investment and vice versa.

The Hash Rate is the CPU power through which miners are currently serving the network. This is usually on a continuous uptrend.

These are just general basic indicators, always think that all models are wrong, but a few are useful.

Here is the bitcoin USD valuation as of February 2022 using weekly candles in a linear chart. The price of BTC, as I recorded this chart, is about $38,000. The 20W EMA is at ca. $45,000 and the 20W SMA is at about $50,000. Technically, at the time of writing, we are in a bear market. The 200W EMA, or actual expected price bottom is at about $26,000. But you can see from past history that BTC price went below it a couple of times, making for historical wealth generation opportunities.

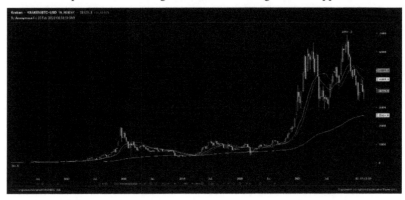

A Logarithmic scale of the same chart using the same indicators offers a more granular view of the price action.

How do I use these charts? Very simple. Whenever the BTC price is at, close or below the 200W MA it is a great time to methodically accumulate BTC. Whenever the BTC is above the bull-market support band and it increases parabolically, it is a good time to skim off just a little bit of my investment.

Please keep in mind that there is no guarantee whatsoever about BTC price's tops and bottoms, and there is no guarantee that BTC will continue to appreciate overtime. Never invest money you will need to cover your living expenses, be aware of tax implications and please consider that this is NO FINANCIAL ADVISE.

A very important on-chain indicator is the hash rate, here shown in both linear and logarithmic scale, source: blockchain.com

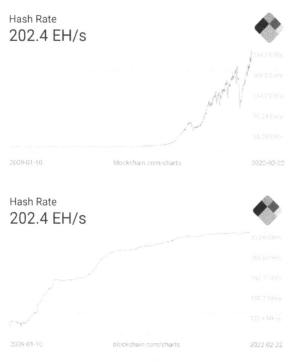

What the hash rate indicators says is that as long as the hash rate keeps on increasing, BTC dollar valuation is also expected to increase. Simply put, for as long as mining companies are willing to invest more and more capital into mining rig and energy, the future of bitcoin looks great.

It is very important to understand investors' psychology to avoid common mistakes. It is very common during bull markets to feel greedy and to FOMO into an investment (FOMO = Fear Of Missing Out). It is also very common to be fearful and to sell coins at a loss or miss out on buying opportunities during bear markets.

Fear & Greed are your enemy and all investors have been victim of it. This is exactly the reason why you should always invest money you can part with and have a long-term horizon. This attitude will allow you to zoom-out, relax and take investment decisions using long-term data and not emotions. If you take this mindset, you will slowly increase your wealth and avoid unnecessary stress.

Smart investors buy and accumulate as many coins as possible during bear markets and only occasionally skim off during times of extreme greed. Furthermore they never buy consumable goods with those hard-to-come gains, they keep some in dry powder, consolidate wealth through physical gold and buy income-generating assets such as real estate, using the generated income to buy consumable goods. That is smart investing, that is generational wealth building.

Let me give you some examples of parabolic growth events when it is so easy to fall for FOMO and capitulations which are times when smart investors buy coins off people victim of fear.

Examples of Parabolic events:

1) Between OCT-2013 and NOV-2013 bitcoin went from $ 103 to $ 1,133 (+ >1,000%)

2) Between NOV-2017 and DEC-2017 bitcoin went from $5,900 to $19,500 (+ >300%)

3) Between MAR-2019 and APR-2021 bitcoin went from $4,800 to $63,000 (+ >1,000%)

Examples of Capitulations:

1) Between 2013 and 2015, bitcoin crumbled from $1,133 down to $172 (- 84%)

2) Between 2017 and 2018, bitcoin crumbled from $19,500 down to $3,200 (-83%)

As you can see it is easy to get excited, but it is just as easy to get turned off by bitcoin unless we deeply understand what bitcoin is and we are able to detach us emotionally from the price and concentrate on the long-term data and take a long-term investment strategy approach.

The mean yearly percentage return during the past 12 years is +156%, range +5,318% // -73%

If we split the averages in 3-year blocks, we have the following total 3-year returns:

2010-2012: +26,920%

2013-2015: +3,084%

2016-2018: +770%

2019-2021: +1,138%

As I report on such life-changing percentage gains, my thoughts go back to 20 months ago when I discussed bitcoin with my bank director. Back then, I asked my bank for a loan which I needed to finance my own home. As part of asking for a loan I had to show assets I held as collateral. As I mentioned bitcoin, he quickly turned cold and told me that bitcoin is nothing short of a scam and that billions were lost by private citizens just in our region during the last few months. The question that I have is very simple, how? Considering the data above, how is it possible to lose money on bitcoin?

The answer is just as simple: only if you day-trade or if buy and sell emotionally motivated by short-term greed and fear.

The other possibility is if you fall victim of scams or lose your private keys.

In day-trading and short-term holding lay the very fallacies which keep people from increasing their wealth by adopting bitcoin.

Traders, on one hand, are nothing short than gamblers as they exchange precious bitcoin back and forth for FIAT, thinking of knowing how the price will develop through technical chart analysis, or even worse, news alerts. This might work for a time, but in the long term, the market will inexorably go against them, and traders will end up on the losing end of the game. Only powerful insiders, whales, and institutions may reliably increase their bitcoin holdings by trading as they are true market-makers and are capable to actively affect the price.

There are also people who have bought and sold bitcoin within a short period of time (which I consider less than three years) because of two reasons, either by confusing spending money with investment money or by buying and selling under FOMO (fear of missing out) and FUD (fear, uncertainty, and doubt). As a rule, Investors should not use money which they need to cover their living expenses as this will sooner or later force them to sell precious Bitcoin under pressure and time constraints. Investors should also not buy under FOMO, or sell out of FUD, as these are losing strategies dictated by emotions. FOMO and FUD (or Fear & Greed) are even skillfully and purposely used to lead unaware investors to transferring cheap coins into the hands of savvy bitcoiners.

Once you start researching and investing in bitcoin, there is one question which everyone asks and which may even quickly become a true obsession, how "high" will bitcoin go in price and by when?

This question comes to mind for two reasons:

1) You want to sell your bitcoin for FIAT in order to buy something
2) You want to sell your bitcoin for FIAT in order to re-buy bitcoin at a cheaper price

The only honest answer I can give is that no one knows. Bitcoin could literally go to zero or to $1.000.000 by the end of 2022, from all I know. These two options are both mathematically possible, although both not very likely. The internet is full of price predictions and theories. My opinion, based on past performance, is that bitcoin will most likely trend higher on a yearly basis, but by diminishing returns as the asset consolidates and matures. Such a growth will also continue to be affected by short-term volatility, albeit also diminishing. How high will it go then? If the current rate continues, if the FED continues to print money and if the adoption keeps on increasing, bitcoin will continue to trend higher until it forces all governments to acquire it as a central reserve asset. It is absolutely possible to see bitcoin over $1,000,000 by 2030 but expect heavy push-backs at the hand of central banks and governments.

If you try to time the market wanting to sell the top and buy the bottom, you will fail! You will never be able to guess the top and the bottom and even if you did you will most likely never be quick enough to act on time.

If you are trying to guess tops and bottoms, you are trading and not investing. My philosophy and my advice to you is to understand bitcoin's intrinsic value, which by pure Darwinism will take over the world. You should then no longer evaluate your portfolio in USD but in bitcoin, or satoshis.

Let me also give you some words of wisdom on life and investing. Becoming financially free takes time, discipline, and commitment. The reason why you will want to become financially free, or financially independent is to be able to have the time and the means to do things for which life is worth living, to grow spiritually, to help less fortunate human beings, to exercise love, which is the greatest force in the universe, to enjoy nature, to spend time with family and friends, to have fun. The steps towards financial freedom and independence are easy if discipline is applied and can be so summarized:

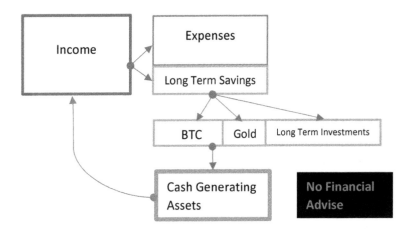

Steps to financial independence, the circle of virtue

1. Spend less than you earn
2. Save in hard sound money which does not devaluate over time, Gold and BTC
3. Invest in cash generating assets: i.e., companies, dividend stocks, real estate
4. Now that your income has increased, increase spending to increase your standards of living and increase savings to generate even bigger investments
5. Repeat

The secret to bitcoin is not to buy low and sell high, the secret of bitcoin is to understand its potential and what it stands for. The secret is to start placing even a small portion of your long-term savings in hard/sound digital money, to use bitcoin in real transactions using the Lightning Network®, to make international remittances through bitcoin, the secret is real adoption.

This is sometimes hard because of the not-always user-friendly technology, because vendors who take bitcoin are still few in most countries, yet things are becoming easier by the day. Stick to it, adopt bitcoin, and join the greatest monetary revolution which will not only improve your wealth, but will free the world.

Chapter seventeen: The Covid pandemic, tyranny and mass social engineering, the weak-up call to freedom and independence

Not the "plague", but it was the governments' overreach, coercion and manipulation which was a true wake-up call for many of us.

Our freedoms have been systematically restricted during the past few decades. Our liberty to interact, to own property, our right to privacy, our right to free speech, our right to bodily autonomy, have all been slowly and systematically eroded.

The Covid pandemic response should not be seen as a single independent episode in history, it truly represents the greatest and latest attack against our individual freedoms, it represents an attack against humanity which could have never been possible without previous life-changing catalyst events such as the JFK's assassination and 9/11. It represents the ultimate fight between good and evil, it will determine if we fall deeper into bondage or if it will spur an age of renaissance.

If indeed Covid-19 was a premediated event with the purpose to further restrict freedoms and introduce a new era of strict social and financial controls, why was it launched in 2019-2020? What was its primary purpose? Were restrictive measures needed to help exit the FIAT debt cycle started in 1971 and transition into a deleveraged new cycle of FIAT money? Was it needed to reassert U.S. financial, political, and military dominance into the 21st century? Was it a necessary catalyst to realize Agenda-2030? Was human depopulation attempted by increasing mortality and decreasing birth rates through a lab virus and gene-therapies? Were these attempts, if at all real, successful?

These are all just questions to a hypothesis, I do not pretend to know the answers, I can only ask these questions and try to associate events with possible motives, I can only try to connect the dots and make sense of all this, knowing that my reasoning could be completely false and knowing that I do not have access to any special classified information, but knowing that my instinct has been right many times before.

With this in mind, it is useful to ponder about some crucial events in recent world history to see if we could frame Covid-19 in such a prospective and evaluate its implication on humanity and freedom today.

Some of these events have always left me doubtful of the official narrative and their unspoken real purpose; Most notably, as already mentioned, the JFK assassination and 9/11 came in mind. Why was JFK assassinated, did Oswald as affirmed by the Warren commission act alone, or was it a conspiracy? And if it was a conspiracy, who was behind it, and why? Wild debates, numerous books and documentaries have been written about this.

The most important question for me is: how did JFK's assassination affect American and world history?

My personal belief is that with JFK's death, free America and the American dream ended. With this event, a new term (very commonly used today) became mainstream to describe people who challenged the official narrative: conspiracy theorist. Ironically, the official narrative cemented with the Warren commission is to many a laughable cover up and the term "conspiracy theorist" has with time become a weaponized pejorative to dismiss dissenting views as non-factual, based on a self-persecutory syndrome, and usually associated with poor and uneducated individuals. While conspiracy theories are just opinions and free interpretation of events, to which everyone is entitled to, some are surely bizarre and blatantly false; Many however, have been proven to be true. In the case of JFK, even 60 years after the event, many documents remain classified, and the official story still sees Oswald as the sole perpetrator. The official story is however clearly a laughable cover up.

Another event which is easily a source of many speculations and "conspiracy theories", and which changed America and the world for ever was 9/11.

Did really high-jackers who barely learned how to pilot small propeller planes in Florida bring down 3 towers in New York using box cutters and two modern passenger planes? My first doubts surfaced as I randomly came across a book by Brigham Young University's professor Steven Jones; Ironically, I graduated from BYU in 1997. Jones was a professor in the physics department and used his academic background to argue that all 3 buildings which collapsed in New York, the two Twin Towers and Building-7, could have never collapsed in such a manner from planes crashing into the buildings. According to him, if I correctly recall his arguments, this could have not been physically possible considering the buildings' steel-frame structures and their melting temperatures. By calculating the buildings' falling speeds, the collapse could only be accounted for if key structural points at the basements of the building had failed in a similar fashion to techniques used in control demolitions. These arguments were scientifically sound, particularly with regards to Building-7, which was never hit by a plane.

If JFK's assassination and 9/11 were inside jobs fruits of conspiracies, what were the motives? And is there a connection between these events and Covid-19?

I cannot tell for sure; a couple of things do come however in my mind; following JFK's assassination the Gold Standard ended, the American government became exponentially larger, and US wars have raged across the globe to protect dollar world domination. I also do know that following 9/11 we saw the American military machine in perpetual full force, particularly in the middle east, and that the Patriot Act started a new era of unprecedented mass civilians' surveillance.

It is for me unquestionable that liberties and freedoms have been heavily lost during the past decades in the name of safety.

Going back to 9/11, which is the event I recall best as I was 25 years old at the time, I remember the heart-breaking images of the collapsing buildings and of innocent people jumping out of windows to escape fire and a painful death. At the time I kept thinking: how did terrorists dare to do all this? For sure this was a new pearl Harbor and justice had to be made.

I remember that during those days and months following the attacks, no-one could even dare to think of challenging the official narrative. Saddam was guilty and had to be attacked, Afghanistan had to be freed of the Taliban and become democratic, Osama had to be found and killed, and freedom-restricting laws had to be passed to stop foreign and domestic terrorism. Whoever dared to hold a different opinion was quickly accused of being anti-patriotic, anti-American, anti-freedom, anti-democracy, and a traitor. Those who questioned the official story of the terrorist attacks in New York and Washington were violently silenced. Those who dared to expose the crimes of the US military and secret services in the years following 9/11, such as Julian Assange and Edward Snowden, received the treatment reserved for terrorists and were imprisoned or forced into exile.

In a very interesting parallel, those who dared to challenge Covid-19's origin narrative, those who dared to challenge lock downs, mandatory inoculations and vax-passports, those who dared to open churches during the pandemic, those who dared to let the unvaxed into restaurants, those who dared to protest in the streets, those who refused to wear masks, had to be declared enemies of the state, enemies of the common good, assassins spreading a virus for the sole egoistic purpose of not accepting "the science" and traitors not worth of living in a free and democratic society. Nobody, after having witnessed all the deaths in New York, after having witnessed the military trucks carrying thousands of bodies out of Bergamo, could dare to challenge authority and stop the slaughter by an invisible deadly enemy for which we have safe and effective remedies: masking, distancing, lock-downs and the Covid-19 vaccines.

How similar was 9/11 and Covid-19 seen in this prospective! Chaos, fear, and madness, powered by unstoppable emotions driven by constant media coverage, which had an apparent simple solution: Bombs for the first, jabs for the second. Both events resulted in an incredible irreversible loss of individual freedoms, and once the dust settles on Covid-19, both will have seen an incredible amount of suffering and loss of human lives.

My professional expertise is in clinical trials, I could write pages and pages about why I think the virus came from gain-of-function activities at the Wuhan institute of virology, where the American intelligence and scientific elites were deeply rooted. I could talk a lot about why the clinical trials responsible for the emergency authorization were, to say the least, suspicious in their handling and statistical analysis. I could complain for hours about the fact that not only dissenting voices were censored, but that over-the-counter safe preventions and cures were blocked, most likely costing the life of hundreds of thousands of people. I could write a lot about why I thought that mRNA genetic material, traveling through nano lipids envelopes into every organ of the body, even across the blood-brain barrier, are a very risky endeavor. I knew very early, as the vax were being released, that these vaccines were not vaccines, but gene therapies camouflaged as such for public acceptance, which could not only stop infection and transmission, but also required multiple shots every 4-6 months with unknown effects on the extremely complex human native immune system. But I am sure you can find better books to learn about all this.

It was a dehumanized world those days, all those people wearing masks walking in fear while keeping distance. Radio, TV and social media urging everyone to protect themselves and others by getting vaccinated. Widespread censorship which I never thought I would see in the western world. The vax centers, with their colorful propaganda posters at their entrances, people freely but fearfully entering the huge inoculation halls, all sitting in silence respecting the 2-meter distance rule, all wearing masks and waiting for their turn to get the jab. It was just all incredibly surreal. I know that the great majority of those people entering the vax hubs had doubts and fears in their minds. Some took the jab because they believed in them, too many did it out of pure convenience, some unfortunately were forced into it by pure coercion. I felt such sadness in my heart seeing all this because I knew that natural immunity protected those who already had the disease, most could have been protected through known pharmaceutical protocols, and I knew that the safety of these gene-therapies could never have been thoroughly tested that fast. Inoculating the world with such a novel technology has been the greatest medical experiment in human history, that is just a fact.

I had even worse feelings when I walked by a vaccination center in Switzerland during a time when parents were first allowed to bring their children to get the jab. Parents had literally fear in their eyes, although I know they were doing it out of conviction of protecting their little ones. One father had tears in his eyes as he brought his little daughter through the entrance. I stood there in silence holding a sign: Unsafe & Ineffective. A police officer stood by me as if I were a criminal, but I was doing it to let naïve people with no notion of how pharmaceuticals work, and how they are tested for safety and effectiveness, that things from the prospective of someone with over a decade of experience in pharmaceutical and medical devices development, did not add up.

Besides the sadness for what I witnessed; it was a tremendous scary time for myself. Not because I was afraid to die, but because I knew they were coming for me, I knew that without the jab I could have not able to work for much longer. My whole family depended on my income, and I could never let them down!

I resisted because I knew it was the right thing to do. I strongly believe that people should be able to take any shot they want, but I also believe that people should be properly informed about benefits, risks and alternatives and be able to take an autonomous and independent medical choice. This is basic medical ethics and human respect, but in the midst of general panic caused by an invisible deadly virus, these principles counted nothing.

The lessons learned by all medical experimentations done during Nazi Germany went all down the drain within weeks.

It was a dark time, but a time which allowed me to understand a lot about the world and made me cherish freedom and self-determination more than anything else on earth.

Freedom of choice is a basic human right which is not negotiable and cannot be put at risk just because we face a crisis. These principles are purposely written in documents such as the constitution and the bill of rights so that we may have guidance in hardship.

I was only able to resist, however, because in the years prior I bought some bitcoin, which I was holding in cold storage. Those assets were supposed to pay off my mortgage, hopefully, but I knew that with them I could survive without work for a few years. Bitcoin allowed me the courage to stand for what is right, the strength to stand for my freedom, the freedom of my children and their future generations.

I stood steadfast, I decided not to bow to tyranny and coercion.

God protected me and my family, my company placed me part-time for only a month and fortunately never got rid of me. I took a hard stance, I made a difficult decision which placed the financial security of my family on the line, but it was the right thing to do.

Governments' behavior and their unison military-style coercive measures have put son against father, wife against husband, employer against employee; these measures fractured society, polarized opinions, and caused health and psychological damage to an incredible amount of people whose effects will be felt for decades to come. I like to say that many lost their lives to the virus, but millions lost their livelihood and their lives to the governments' measures.

But why did so many people allow their government to take their freedom away so easily? If just a small percentage, 20-30% of the population had opposed tyranny, my life and my right to free choice would have been much easier to assert. Why do people value freedom so little? Are people not understanding what is happening to them, or are people just mentally weak?

If we look at the origins of modern society, which according to my very personal opinion started with the end of World War II, the role of government used to be much smaller, taxation was only a fraction of what it is today, and regulations were far fewer. Health, safety, political crises, wars, and wars on terrorism have all been commonly used to both increase taxes, enlarge governments, promote wars, and require ever more regulations with the inevitable result of restricting personal freedoms. Human conditioning, social engineering, and restrictions on freedom was done slowly yet systematically. It was like cooking a frog in slow heat, the frog would get used to the temperature and never escape.

Today it is not only expected that you would wear a seat belt or wear a bicycle helmet; although if you think about it, as you pay your health insurance it is really your choice if you want to put yourself in danger or not. But it is expected and normal to give up all your data, be tracked anytime and anywhere through your smart phone, allow cameras to use facial recognition, accept facial masking, give up bodily autonomy and freedom of medical choice in exchange for safety and, ironically, freedom.

But we are not either safe or free, we are just slaves of the matrix!

People should learn principles of freedom, self-esteem, self-reliance at home and in school. But they don't. People learn in school to obey and are rewarded if they do and are punished if they don't, in a social behavioral shaping mechanism which reminds me of Pavlov's dogs. This is the crude reality in our democratic free world.

What is the connection between JFK, 9/11, Covid-19 and bitcoin? Why have I decided to talk about this in this book?

All these events have had the net result to restricting our freedoms. The Covid-19 coordinated government response are the last 100 meters of a long marathon. There are a multitude of factors that probably triggered such a vile and coward attack. The end of a FIAT debt cycle, the zeal to protect US world monetary and military supremacy, and the dystopian woke/globalist vision of a raceless, nationless, sexless world which promotes diversity on paper when in reality flattens everything through ideological violence and pure dystopia.

Something is sure, all these measures could have only been implemented through the FIAT money system; but maybe, all this is also happening to protect the FIAT money system.

This is why I hold and use bitcoin. It allowed me to increase my wealth and self-reliance to resist tyranny, it allows me to move all my belongings across the globe by carrying a simple USB stick or by memorizing my private keys, it allows me freedom of speech, freedom of movement and freedom of choice.

I think, therefore I am; but I also choose, therefore I am.

Many people accepted the jab because they were fearful, many because they believed in "the science", but the majority took it because they could not afford to and/or they did not have the courage to stand up. All of them, regardless of what they believed, were played. All of us were treated like nothing more than human cattle.

Bitcoin is my ticket to freedom, and it is time that we all retake our freedoms back.

We are conditioned and trained since birth, we fall in debt and work all our lives trying to repay it, we are taxed so heavily that most of us end-up working mostly for the government, we live in fear of not making ends meet and to lose what we have already acquired; We are given fake money which devaluates in value and, to top it all off, we fall deeper and deeper in total institutionalized control.

Money has been weaponized; cash has been heavily restricted through the usual narratives of money laundering and illicit acts. CBDCs will soon provide the final tools for complete and utter control, particularly once associated with the use of a social credit score mechanism.

However, it is technology itself which is coming to the rescue. It allows us the freedom to own, save and spend our own money. Bitcoin and the blockchain revolution are formidable tools to regain personal freedoms and self-determination. This is the very reason I am writing this book, not to teach you how to get rich, but to teach you to break off the chains of tyranny and exercise your freedom, your self-reliance and regain your dignity... It is about time!

As money is louder than anything, cast your vote with money! Exit FIAT and enter bitcoin! You do not have to adopt much to make a difference, a few sats in self-custody make you already that much more sovereign.

The pandemic was the worse time of my life in a lot of ways. Not so much the virus, which was definitely dangerous and in my personal opinion synthetically generated, but the brute force of governments coming for my body, coming for my family, coming to destroy me if I did not exactly do what they told me to do. It has been, however, such a weak-up call that this was also a time which I will cherish in gratitude forever.

Covid-19 is an incredible last attack against humanity, made possible by the slow yet systematic erosion of personal freedoms, and the FIAT money system. None of all this could have ever happened without money printed out of thin air and the huge governmental, military, and non-governmental apparatus that all this fake money is able to create.

This is why I wrote this book, because only sound money can re-establish free sovereign individuals and free sovereign nations.

After this pandemic I am a different person, a better person. Carbon if compressed enough will generate diamonds, and this is exactly what has happened to so many of us. We have become diamonds and learned to exercise the strongest force in the universe, love, which is light.

Bitcoin is the financial power of the sun to grant us freedom, equality, and the right to happiness.

Chapter eighteen: Conclusions

"What if I told you the only way to escape the matrix is to unlearn everything that you have been taught and rebuild your entire belief system based on critical thought and analysis"?

This book has been a huge learning experience for me, it took about 14 months of researching, writing, and editing to bring you this work.

The FIAT money system is built on debt and requires infinite more debt to function. It can literally be compared to heroin, it gives you a high, but to function you require more and more of it until you eventually die, unless you are able to escape it, which is extremely hard.

This system of money printed out of thin air, by decree, constitutes the greatest earthly power and is reserved for a handful of individuals and organizations who are the ones who truly control the world.

In just a few decades, the FIAT money system, coupled with technological advancements and readily available cheap energy, has allowed for incredible economic growth and unparalleled change. However, it is also responsible for exploitation, enslavement, ever-growing disparities, poverty, economic, physical and biological warfare, political divide, the cancerous growth of government, the endless growth of armies and secret services, and the indiscriminate pollution of the planet.

The world will never, nor was it ever meant to be perfect. But the FIAT money system guarantees inequality by giving the very few the power to decide on the very many and requires ever more control to stay afloat. A true market economy gives equal opportunities to all, it allows supply and demand to manage society through natural equilibrium, requires minimal government intervention, automatic small military budgets and guarantees peace and prosperity through fair trade.

But a true market economy requires an independent and finite medium of exchange.

Traditionally, the only way to do so was to tie the money supply to gold. Gold has been in fact real money for thousands of years, first because it is rare, second because it is just a beautiful looking metal with many use cases. But there is nothing magical about gold, it is just a tool to keep the printing press, and the powers associated with it, in check.

In today's technologically driven world where almost everything is becoming digital, we need a digitally native tool to bring back sound money. You need a digital asset that has the monetary qualities of gold but that can be digitally operated.

This can only be bitcoin.

Going back to hard-sound money requires a revolution, for the simple reason that those in power will never freely relinquish it.

Bitcoin could be the first revolution in human history which did not require the firing of a single bullet. This revolution can be fought at the individual and the governmental level.

At the individual level it is enough to exchange a small portion of your savings into bitcoin and keep it in self custody.

At the state level it requires legislation making bitcoin legal tender and a treasury reserve, but it also requires governments to relinquish their powers by going on a bitcoin standard, which is de facto separation of money and state.

While for an individual is after all an easy step, for nation states things are much more complex. First because those in power lose most of it by relinquishing the printing press, second because it has international implications which are not that easy to unwind. However, this is becoming a possibility as small third-world countries are becoming willing to do so, and because wars are pushing large state actors to take strategic financial warfare steps. Two examples which come in mind are El Salvador, a third world country which has little to lose and much to gain by adopting bitcoin, and Russia who first banned bitcoin mining just as I started this book, and now as I write this final chapter in January 2023, is even considering adopting bitcoin and bitcoin mining to counter its financial isolation brought by its war with NATO. Interestingly, I predicted this at the beginning of the book, which was written well before war with Russia broke out.

Bitcoin guarantees private property rights, fair rules, and opportunities for everyone. Bitcoin is true decentralization of power and therefore true democracy. Bitcoin is economic freedom in its deepest form.

Bitcoin was built for our times, it unleashed blockchain technological developments which has changed the world in a way which can never be reversed.

I do not know if bitcoin will go to zero, or if it will be incredibly valuable as it becomes a world reserve asset. However history will play out, I hope that through this book you were able to gain more knowledge and you will feel motivated to strive and achieve more freedom and self-determination.

Slowly but surely, you have periodically given up small pieces of freedom; but at the end, you have been left with no freedom and a backpack full of perceived safety. It is time to change that, it is time to take control and responsibility back in our hands.

Political choice is an illusion created between those with power and those without, many still believe that by casting a vote you are choosing your own future. But that is pure fantasy, you are given different choices of the same thing. This is the very reason why in western democracies less and less people go to vote with every election which goes by. Today there is a way for you to cast your vote in a meaningful way again, and that is by adopting bitcoin. Buy some sats, keep them in self custody, spend some if you know a vendor who accepts it, and make your voice count. Money talks, exit FIAT!

I wrote this book during incredibly tough times when I was locked in my house and providing for my family was threatened by truly evil forces.

This is a testament to myself, my family and humanity that:

this life is only worth living if lived free!

Roberto de Filippo

www.satoshi-lab.org

We started the book with a quote of Albert Einstein about love. Let me finish the book with more quotes attributed to Albert Einstein. These are thought he wrote to his daughter and help me find inspiration and guidance in life:

About Science:

"As far as the laws of mathematics refer to reality, they are not certain; and as far as they are certain, they do not refer to reality."

"One thing I have learned in a long life: that all our science, measured against reality, is primitive and childlike — and yet it is the most precious thing we have."

About the common good and individuality:

"It is important for the common good to foster individuality: for only the individual can produce the new ideas which the community needs for its continuous improvement and requirements — indeed, to avoid sterility and petrifaction."

Title | Bitcoin and the ultimate fight for freedom
Author | Roberto de Filippo
ISBN | 979-12-21459-28-9

Youcanprint
Via Marco Biagi 6, 73100 Lecce
www.youcanprint.it
info@youcanprint.it

Youcanprint
Printed in January 2023